ENGLISH USAGE GUIDE

Also by Derek Richter:
Life in Research

ENGLISH USAGE GUIDE

Derek Richter

The Book Guild Ltd
Sussex England

The Book Guild Ltd.
25 High Street,
Lewes, Sussex

First published 1992
© Derek Richter 1992

Set in Baskerville
Type setting by Kudos Graphics
Slinfold, West Sussex
Printed in Great Britain by
Antony Rowe Ltd.
Chippenham, Wiltshire.

A catalogue record for this book is
available from the British Library

ISBN 0 86332 738 9

CONTENTS

ACKNOWLEDGEMENTS

I wish to thank the English language teacher Antony Markoff and the Director-General of the English-Speaking Union, David Hicks MBE for their help in preparing this book.

I also wish to thank the authors and publishers who have kindly given permission to include quotations from the following copyright publications. 'Mad dogs and English-men' (Copyright Noel Coward Estate 1932) reprinted by permission of Michael Imison Playrights Ltd. 'Concept of Mind' (Gilbert Ryle); permission of the Principal and Fellows of Hertford College. Motoring News; News Publications Ltd. 'Statisitical Tables for Biological, Agriculture and Medical Research' (Fisher & Yates) published by Oliver & Boyd; permission of Longman Group UK Ltd. 'Homosynaptic testing . . .' (Granit and Job) J. Neurophysiol.; The American Physiological Society. 'Traumatic fractures . . .' (C. H. Marsh); The Royal Society of Medicine. The Sunday Express; Express Newspapers plc. The British Medical Journal; The British Medical Association. The Guardian; Guardian News Service Ltd. 'Hopkins and Biochemistry' (Ed. Joseph Needham); W. Heffer & Sons Ltd. 'The complete poems of W. H. Davies'; Jonathon Cape Ltd; Lampen and Wang (J. Biol. Chem.); The American Society of Biochemistry and Molecular Biology; 'The Soldier' (Rupert Brooke); Sidgwick & Jackson.

FOREWORD

Educated people who speak good English are sometimes surprised to find that they have difficulty in communicating easily with people from other backgrounds who speak a slightly different type of English. That applies not only to those who have come from different countries, but also to people who work in different academic, cultural or business fields. Problems of communication often arise at international meetings at which English is the language used, and misunderstandings are not uncommon in the discussion of technical, scientific, medical or business matters. The account given here is intended to help communication by clarifying the meaning of some of the different types of English that are used.

1

INTRODUCTION

How did the English language come into being? A language is not just a collection of words and grammar: it is a means of communicating thoughts, feelings and ideas. It is built up slowly over a long period of time by people who want to make contact with each other and who wish to share each other's ways of thinking and seeing the world they live in.

English started originally as the language of the people living in England, and it owes its character partly to the fact that they were a mixed population which had come from several different regions, including those now known as France, Germany, the Netherlands, Scandinavia and the Mediterranean countries. During long periods when French was the language of the aristocracy and of the King's Court, English developed as the language of the common people. From time to time scholars tried to help by defining rules of grammar and spelling, but the English were never very good at keeping to the rules, and gradually the language took on a simpler form and became less complex than many other languages. The success of the English language in spreading throughout the world depends in part on the fact that English suits the needs of the common people in being relatively simple. That also makes it easier to learn. Spoken by only about five and a half millions in 1600, English is now spoken by some six hundred millions in the British Isles, North America, Australia, India, Africa and other parts of the world.

Another thing that has added to the acceptance of the English language is the readiness of the English people to receive words and ideas from other languages. To the French it is indebted for many common words such as *menu, cream, café, dinner, madam* and *toilet*. Other useful words have come into English from many other languages including Persian, Hindi, Arabic and Haitian. However, if we wish to communicate satisfactorily with people brought up in other cultures, we need something more than a vocabulary of words. We need to have some understanding of their basic philosophy and the ways in which their attitudes and viewpoints differ from our own. We should also understand their types of humour.

One way in which a language becomes established is through the little sayings called proverbs which persist down the centuries, and which are repeated by one generation after another because they express in a neat way something that ordinary people want to say. The words that are used in the proverbs gain special value because through frequent repetition they become well-known to all. This is true also to some extent of some often-quoted passages in books, some sayings of famous men, a few well-known poems and some lines from popular songs. A number of items of this kind are collected together in the following sections of this book. Can the discerning reader find in them any clues to the attitudes and characteristic ways of thinking of people in the English-speaking world?

What is known as the Common Language is broadly similar right round the world, but there are some minor differences in the names given to common objects in the different countries in which English is spoken, and that is soon apparent to the visitor who arrives in one country from another. Thus the structure used at many airports and known in the USA as the 'elevator' is generally known in England as the 'lift'. Similarly the toilet, known in the USA as the 'wash-room', is known in England as the 'loo'. There are even differences in denoting the time, and it can be a surprise to the visitor to hear the Americans call 'half-eleven' what the English know better as 'half past ten'.

Different to some extent from the English taught in the schools is the kind of language commonly used by English people in their homes. That is something which it can also be helpful for visitors from other countries to understand.

2

ENGLISH SPOKEN IN THE HOME

Much of the language spoken by the people in English-speaking countries is not of the kind that is learned at school, but language acquired in the course of family life at home. Young children pick up words and phrases from their parents and in talking to each other. Their language is also influenced by the traditional nursery rhymes and popular songs they may hear. These vary to some extent in different places. Some common examples are as follows:

1. Jack and Jill went up the hill
    To fetch a pail of water,
    Jack fell down and broke his crown,
    And Jill came tumbling after.

2. There was a little girl,
    And she had a little curl
    Right in the middle of her forehead.
    And when she was good
    She was very, very good,
    And when she was bad she was horrid.

3. The grand old Duke of York
    He had ten thousand men.
    He marched them up to the top of the hill,
    And he marched them down again.
    And when they were up they were up,
    And when they were down they were down,
    And when they were only half way up
    They were neither up nor down.

4.   Humpty Dumpty sat on a wall,
        Humpty Dumpty had a great fall.
        All the King's horses and all the King's men
        Couldn't put Humpty together again.

5.   We watch the trains come in,
        We hear the porters shout.
        And after we've watched the trains come in,
        We watch the trains go out.

6.   One for sorrow,
        Two for joy,
        Three for a girl,
        Four for a boy,
        Five for silver,
        Six for gold,
        Seven for something
        That's never been told.

7.   Boys and girls come out to play.
        The moon is shining bright as day.
        Come with a whoop and come with a call.
        Come with goodwill or not at all.

8.   'To bed! To bed!' says Sleepy-head,
        But 'Wait awhile,' says Slow.
        'Put on the pot,' says Hungry-one,
        'We'll sup before we go'.

9.   My mother says I never should
        Play with the gypsies in the wood.
        If I did she would say,
        'Naughty little girl to disobey'.

One of the games that children play when they are together is that of asking each other riddles. A riddle is a puzzling question, generally with an unexpected answer, as in the following examples:

10. **Question:** What's round as a biscuit,
                  Busy as a bee;

                        The prettiest little thing
                        You ever did see?
        Answer: A watch.
11. **Question:** Who ran to help me when I fell,
                        And kissed the place to make it well?
        Answer: Mother.
12. **Question:** When is an Englishman's house *not* his
                        castle?
        Answer: When his wife's around.

BIRTHDAY PARTIES

When one of the members of a family has a birthday, it is
customary for them to meet together with a few friends to
celebrate. Generally they bring presents for the person who
has the birthday and he or she may also receive birthday
cards wishing them many happy returns of the day. A
birthday card usually has an attractive picture on the front,
and on the back or inside there may be a simple verse:

13.   'I hope you'll have the NICEST day
        A boy like you could spend.
        A day so full of FUN, you'll wish
        That it will never end.'

At the birthday celebration they then enjoy the special
food and drink which are brought out for the occasion, and
they may express their good wishes by singing a little song,
which for a girl named Caroline would run:

14.   'Happy birthday to you! Happy birthday to you!
        Happy birthday dear Caroline!
        Happy birthday to you!'

After the meal they may sing more songs or dance and
play games. They may also invite some of the children to
recite verses. On such occasions they sometimes recite
nonsense verses or poems of a humorous kind that make
them all laugh:

15.   I'm busy doing nothing;
    Working the whole day through
    Trying hard to find
    Lots of things not to do.

    I'm busy going nowhere;
    Isn't it just a crime?
    I'd like to be unhappy,
    But I never have the time!

16.   Sing a song of sixpence,
        A bagful of rye;
    Four and twenty blackbirds,
        Baked in a pie.
    And when the pie was opened,
        The birds began to sing,
    And was not that a dainty dish
        To set before a king?

    The king was in the parlour,
        Counting out his money;
    The queen was in the kitchen,
        Eating bread and honey;
    The maid was in the garden,
        Laying out the clothes,
    Up came a magpie
        And bit off her nose.

                              (Anon.)

17.   'You are old Father William,' the young man said,
        'And your hair has become very white;
    And yet you incessantly stand on your head –
        Do you think, at your age, it is right?'

    'In my youth,' Father William replied to his son,
        'I feared it might injure the brain;
    But now that I'm perfectly sure I have none,
        Why, I do it again and again.'

                        (Lewis Carroll)

The older members of the family generally engage in conversation with their friends, but it is said that the English do not like to discuss politics, which can arouse ill-feeling, or religion, which can be a source of disagreement, or sex, which is felt to be impolite. So the only thing left to talk about is the weather, about which they always complain. However, they also like to talk about their gardens, their pets, and, in the country, about their farms. They are also fond of discussing sports such as football, cricket or other ball games.

Besides birthdays, most families have some sort of celebration on Christmas Day. In the United States celebrations are held on Independence Day, and in Scotland on New Year's Eve (31st December).

Popular songs have played a part in keeping in circulation certain words and phrases.

18.   Daisy, Daisy,
Give me your answer, do!
I'm quite crazy,
All for the love of you.
It won't be a stylish marriage:
I can't afford a carriage.
But you'd look sweet
Upon the seat of a bicycle made for two.

19.   As I sat on a sunny bank,
A sunny bank, a sunny bank,
As I sat on a sunny bank
On Christmas Day in the morning.

I saw three ships come sailing by,
Come sailing by, come sailing by,
I saw three ships come sailing by,
On Christmas Day in the morning.

(Anon.)

20.   Show me the way to go home.
I'm tired and I want to go to bed,
I had a little drink an hour ago,
And it's gone right to my head.

21.   Let him go. Let him tarry.
Let him sink or let him swim.
For he doesn't care for me
And I don't care for him.

He can go and find another
Whom I hope he will enjoy.
For I'm going to marry
A far, far nicer boy.

22.   Mad dogs and Englishmen
Go out in the midday sun;
The Japanese don't care to,
The Chinese wouldn't dare to;
Hindus and Argentines
Sleep firmly from twelve to one,
But Englishmen detest a siesta.
In the Philippines
There are lovely screens
To protect you from the glare.
In the Malay States
There are hats like plates
Which the Britishers won't wear.
At twelve noon
The natives swoon
And no further work is done,
But mad dogs and Englishmen
Go out in the midday sun.

It seems such a shame
When the English claim
The earth
That they give rise to such hilarity and mirth.

(Noel Coward)

3

PROVERBS AND OTHER SAYINGS

What kinds of thoughts do we find in the ordinary language of the people who grew up in England in the past? Some old sayings express the kind of everyday wisdom known as common sense. Many of them deal with how people behave, or ought to behave, under different conditions: they express a simple philosophy that may help people to deal with the problems with which they are faced.

1. You cannot have your cake and eat it too.
2. As you make your bed, so you must lie on it.
3. If a thing is worth doing, it is worth doing well.
4. What's done is not to do.
5. It is better late than never.
6. God helps those who help themselves.
7. The road to hell is paved with good intentions.
8. It is a long road that has no ending.
9. It is never too late to mend.
10. Nothing ventured, nothing gained.
11. Where there's a will, there's always a way.
12. When in Rome, do as the Romans do.
13. What can't be cured must be endured.
14. No-one is called on to suffer more than he is able to bear.
15. The back is made for the burden.
16. All work and no play makes Jack a dull boy.
17. Patience is a virtue.
    Possess it if you can.
    It's sometimes found in women,
    But never in a man!
18. One good turn deserves another.

19. A friend in need is a friend indeed.
20. Great minds think alike, but fools rarely differ.
21. The best help is not to harm.
22. Two wrongs do not make a right.
23. There is no rest for the wicked.
24. It is an ill wind that blows nobody any good.
25. It takes a strong man to be always gentle and kind.
26. Early to bed and early to rise,
    Makes a man healthy, wealthy and wise.
27. People who live in glass houses should not throw stones.
28. It is easy to be wise after the event.
29. You may think you know best, but you cannot live other people's lives for them.
30. A Jack of all trades is master of none.
31. A little knowledge is a dangerous thing.
32. Time and tide wait for no man.
33. Set a thief to catch a thief.
34. Beggars cannot be choosers.
35. Out of the frying-pan, into the fire.
36. What the eye does not see, the heart does not grieve over.
37. Sticks and stones can break your bones,
    But names need never hurt you.
38. Don't cross your bridges before you get to them.
39. A man must cut his coat according to his cloth.
40. If at first you don't succeed,
    Try, try, try again.
41. The bad workman blames his tools.
42. The higher you fly, the harder you fall.
43. No news is good news.
44. All's well that ends well.

The English are said to be exceptionally fond of animals, and there are many proverbs in which they are mentioned.

45. Every dog has his day.
46. You can take a horse to water, but you cannot make it drink.
47. A bird in the hand is worth two in the bush.
48. Let sleeping dogs lie.

49. You cannot fool an old bird with chaff.
50. Do not look a gift-horse in the mouth.
51. A cat may look at a king.
52. A leopard does not change its spots.
53. You can give a dog a bad name and hang him.
54. You cannot teach an old dog new tricks.
55. Do not keep a dog and bark yourself.

A number of proverbs and popular sayings use illustrations taken from the domestic scene.

56. The test of the pudding is in the eating.
57. The watched pot never boils.
58. If you don't like the heat, don't stay in the kitchen.
59. Don't throw out the baby with the bath water.
60. Too many cooks spoil the broth.
61. An apple a day keeps the doctor away.
62. If you don't like my apples, don't shake my tree.
63. It's jam yesterday, jam tomorrow,
    But never, never jam today.
64. Do not bite off more than you can chew.
65. Enough is as good as a feast.

Expressions from the proverbs are often used by public speakers and by writers in the popular press. 'Proverbs are the philosophy of the common people,' wrote Francis Bacon nearly four centuries ago. Some acquaintance with the proverbs can therefore help us to understand people's ways of thinking as well as helping us to get the full sense of what they may be trying to say. It may be noted that the meaning of a proverb may depend not only on the context in which it is used but also on the way in which the words are spoken. Thus in some contexts the proverb 'Boys will be boys' is spoken in such a way as to convey the meaning 'Young men cannot resist being naughty boys'.

A proverb is often used to express an opinion because its blunt simplicity or overstatement can bring a touch of humour into a statement which otherwise would be troublesome or boring.

4

MEANINGFUL QUOTATIONS

Further evidence of the ways of thinking of English-speaking people is to be found in the sayings and writings of their writers and famous men. Some of the following quotations are well-known:

1. 'England expects that every man this day will do his duty.'

    (Lord Nelson)

2. 'We hold these truths to be self-evident, that all men are created equal, that they are endowed by their Creator with certain unalienable Rights, that among these are Life, Liberty and the pursuit of Happiness. That to secure these rights, Governments are instituted among Men, deriving their just powers from the consent of the governed. That whenever any form of Government becomes destructive of these ends, it is the Right of the People to alter or to abolish it, and to institute new Government, laying its foundations on such principles and organizing its powers in such form, as to them shall seem most likely to effect their Safety and Happiness.'

    (Jefferson)

3. 'What's the bloom and the texture of the skin,
   Compared with peace of mind and harmony within?'

    (Robert Burns)

4. 'One crowded hour of glorious life

Is worth an age without a name.'

(Shelley)

5. 'It is by the Goodness of God that we have in our country three unspeakably precious things: freedom of speech, freedom of conscience and the prudence never to practise either.'

(Mark Twain)

6. 'To travel hopefully is better than to arrive,
And the true success is labour.'

(R.L. Stevenson)

7. 'If a man hasn't found something he will die for, he isn't fit to live.'

(Martin Luther King)

8. 'Never in the field of human conflict was so much owed by so many to so few.'

(Churchill)

9. 'A thing of beauty is a joy forever:
Its loveliness increases; it will never
Pass into nothingness,'

(Keats)

10. 'You can fool all of the people some of the time, and some of the people all the time, but you cannot fool all the people all of the time.'

(Abraham Lincoln)

11. 'A rose by any other name would smell as sweet.'
(Shakespeare)

12. 'The ultimate test of morality for each individual is to be found in how he leaves others whom he encounters individually. The test for all of us is whether the lives of those we meet are better for their having met us, or whether they are worse.'

(Ronald Butt)

13. 'Power corrupts. Absolute power corrupts absolutely.'
(Lord Acton)

14. 'Never meet violence with violence. Show understanding, and then a little kindness helps.'
(Fisher)

15. 'What the English like is something they can beat time to, something that hits them straight in the drum of the ear.'
(Handel)

16. For what we are about to receive may the Lord make us truly grateful.
(A traditional grace)

17. 'The quality of mercy is twice bless'd;
It blesseth him that gives and him that takes.'
(Shakespeare)

18. 'Doing nothing, that's death. Helping people, that is life.'
(Oxfam)

19. 'Don't wait for fair weather, which never was and never will be, but gathering such scattered method as you can command, press forward towards your goal.'
(Davy Jones)

20. 'The more I study, the more I know.
The more I know, the more I forget.
The more I forget, the less I know.
Then why study?'

21. 'It is alright to be bad if you are beautiful.'

22. 'After all is said and done, there is a lot more said than done.'

23. 'Progress is only made by the adoption of ideas very different from those current at the time.'

(Selye)

24. 'If a man will begin with certainties, he shall end in doubts; but if he will be content to begin with doubts, he shall end in certainties.'

(Francis Bacon)

25. 'Prove all things; hold fast that which is good.'

(Thessalonian)

26. Grant me the sense to accept the things I cannot change, the courage to change those that I can, and the wisdom to know the difference.

(Nun's Prayer)

Some quotations from countries with other languages have found a home in the English language.

27. 'I disagree with everything you say, but I will defend with my life your right to say it.'

(Voltaire)

28. 'Man is born free, and everywhere he is in chains.'

(Rousseau)

29. 'A country governed by the working class is like a household ruled by the nursery.'

(Otto von Bismarck)

30. 'Since wars arise in the minds of men, it is in the minds of men that the defences of peace must be constructed.'

(UNESCO Constitution)

31. 'There are still people who blush to have a body.'

(De Gourmont)

There are many well-known verses and sayings that relate to affairs of the heart.

32. 'It is love that makes the world go round.'

33. 'Faint heart never won fair lady!'

34. 'The course of true love never did run smooth.'
(Shakespeare)

35. 'Tis better to have loved and lost
Than never to have loved at all.'
(Tennyson)

36. 'In the spring a young man's fancy lightly turns to thoughts of love.'
(Tennyson)

5

DIFFERENT VARIETIES OF ENGLISH

No language is uniformly the same in every place where it is spoken. It is not hard to pick out differences in the English heard in different localities; we may compare for example the English of Cape Town, Wisconsin, Dublin, Calcutta and Hong Kong. Even in an island as small as Britain there are striking differences in the words and idioms heard in the fishing villages around the coast, in the mining valleys and in the workshops, farmlands and towns. In the course of history the language of the English Court has always differed more or less from that of the rest of the people, and social differences in the use of words can be detected even today. Distinctive variations can be heard again in the intellectual tones sometimes heard in the British Broadcasting Corporation's Third Programme, in the cautious restraint of the bishop's parlour and in the racy language of the turf.

The English used in writing differs everywhere from the colloquial or spoken language, and here again special varieties are used for purposes such as writing verses, business letters, scientific articles, legal documents and religious tracts. It is clear that English is not really a single uniform language, but it is made up of a large number of partly isolated pockets, each with their own special selection of technical words and customary forms of speech. These separate pockets are linked together by a system of essential words and structures, common to them all and known as the *common language*.

There is a continuous exchange of words between the common language and the various specialised departments. It often happens, for example, that a new slang-word gains in popularity and becomes widely used in certain departments in the English speaking world. Many of these slang-words are happily short-lived, but sometimes they are found to fulfil a special need (*mob, jazz, movie, radio, bus*), and then through their general acceptance they gradually cease to be slang. Usage is, after all, the only ultimate test of the 'correctness' of a word.

It is easy to find examples of bad English in contemporary writing. It is often seen for example in business letters and in the kinds of writing commonly known as 'journalese', 'officialese', or 'pudder', of which examples have been collected by Quiller-Couch, Gowers and Ivor Brown. The following examples of current English writing are intended, not as specimens of bad English, but to illustrate the extent of variation in the language used in specialised departments of different kinds. Each of the passages quoted is perfectly clear to anyone familiar with the department in which it is used, but anyone unfamiliar with the specialised field might have some difficulty in understanding the meaning straight away.

(a) 'Aristotle realised that in talking about motives we are talking about dispositions of a certain sort, a sort different from competences; he realised too that any motive, unlike any competence, is a propensity of which it is sense to say that in a given man in a given walk of life this motive is too strong, too weak, or neither too strong, nor too weak.'

This passage is an example of the language used by philosophers: it is from Gilbert Ryle's book *The Concept of Mind* (1949). It illustrates the value of Latin words, which are not inappropriate in writing of this kind.

(b) 'The pyrimidine nucleosidase is stable only in the presence of divalent anions, whereas the purine nucleosidase is stable in tri(hydroxy-methyl)-aminomethane-HCl buffer, but rapidly becomes inactive in phosphate or arsenate buffers. This differential stability of the enzymes is

26

probably the basis of the apparent stimulatory or inhibitory effects of divalent anions.'

Passage (b) is a straightforward specimen of scientific writing from an American periodical *The Journal of Biological Chemistry*. It gives some examples of the names of chemical substances.

(c) 'Recently there has been rather more institutional switching within the medium-dated group, with Funds generally going a little longer. From time to time, for policy reasons, some institutions have even been switching out to the longer.'

Passage (c) is from the *Financial Times*.

(d) 'Unbolt the tappet blocks and prise off their dowels. The tappets are restrained from falling out of the tappet blocks by circlips fitted around their upper ends, and will come away with the tappet blocks. Remove the sump, timing chain case, timing chain and sprockets. Extract the dowel screws securing the centre camshaft bearings to the block and remove the front thrust plate.'

Passage (d) is a specimen of engineering language from *Motoring*.

(e) 'A cyclic or dicyclic substitution which gives an incomplete block solution will also give the corresponding Youden square, provided that each block is written in the order in which it is generated. The complementary Youden square solution may be obtained by performing the same cyclic substitution on the block which is complementary to the given block. Cyclic solutions in two families provide an extension of Youden squares.'

Mathematical writing is apt to be so full of formulae that it is practically impossible for any non-mathematical reader to follow it: but (e) is a comparatively mild specimen from the *Statistical Tables* of Fisher and Yates. The common words *block* and *family* are used here as technical terms with a restricted meaning.

(f) 'The way to the coal face is low and narrow and badly lighted. It is made by cutting away a bed of coal. When a way is cut through the coal, it is roofed with supports of wood. These keep the great mass of earth and stone on top of the mine from falling in the heads of the miners.'

Passage (f) may be contrasted with the previous examples in being eminently simple and clear. It deals with mining, a specialised field which has more than a thousand special technical terms; but this passage is in Basic English, which is largely taken from the common language, so that almost anyone can understand it. Note the use of *lighted* instead of the more usual irregular formation *lit*. It is taken from *Basic English for Polish Students* by C. Halpen.

(g) 'The *Scherzo polimetrico* is a moto perpetuo movement in D major. The speed is an unvarying *vivace*, except for a *presto coda*, and the triplet figure is all-pervasive. The bar-lines, however, rarely coincide in all instruments, and where they do so the effect of uniformity of length is cancelled out by unsymmetrical happenings *inside* the bar.'

Passage (g) is easily recognised as the musicians' language from the Italian terms which are used. The Italian terms provide a kind of international language understood by musicians in every part of the world.

(h) 'Homosynaptic testing is complicated because of the combination of fringe testing with effects of depression (refratoriness and subnormality) in the motoneurones that have fired. The amount of firing must be considered. If negligible, there may

28

be very little difference between homo- and hetero-synaptic testing in stretch, as often is seen with Dial cats. There is generally more firing in decerebrate cats.'

Passage (h) is an example of the physiologists' language: it is from the *Journal of Neurophysiology*. The word *fire* is given here a special technical meaning which the layman would hardly suspect.

(i) 'Here, in pale silk organdie and floating ostrich feather fronds, in trailing yellow chiffon with fringed primrose shawl, languor became a positive quality - creating a new sort of woman, exquisite, enchanting and slightly out of this world. In daylight, still ethereal, she may wear a simple tailored suit of heavy white lace over coffee poult.'

Passage (i) is from a fashion article in a daily newspaper. The language of clothes and cookery is as technical as any to those who are not familiar with it.

(j) 'There is no difference in the mitotic and meiotic processes of transmission of alleles with dominant or recessive, intermediate or additive effects: but, since phenotypes, not genotypes, are the objects of observation, the presence or absence, the disappearances and the reappearances of traits follow different rules depending on the type of the controlling allele. The developmental difference which is the basis of dominance and recessiveness, becomes expressed in dominant and recessive hereditary transmissive phenotypes.'

Passage (j) gives a further example of scientific writing from a book by C Stern entitled *Human Genetics*. The layman might put the three scientific passages (b), (h) and (j) together as all are rather difficult for him to follow and representing a single scientific language: he will probably not suspect that a chemist who can understand passage (b) with ease might have great difficulty in understanding (h) in physiology and (j) in genetics, and vice versa. Science is now so much divided into small specialised branches that it is often hard for a worker in one branch to understand the language of another. In the words of Andrade: 'we no longer have men of learning writing for other men of learning, or men of science writing for other men of science ... but infra-red spectroscopists writing for other infra-red spectroscopists – and very soon they will have a journal of their own.'

(k) 'Time and again in that storming Preston opening he flutter-footed his way down the right wing with that peculiar flowing left-footed dribble. There was no stopping Preston's Flying Plumber. Ask Ronnie Burgess and Arthur Willis. They were practically turning inside out. Feeding Finney was a brilliant young man, Jimmy Baxter, at inside left, with Charlie Wayman helping the flow of passes. Yet it was the amazing Withers who stole North End's thunder and nearly won this match of the day for Tottenham. In the fourth minute Spurs, with the gale whistling like a banshee behind them, faced a corner so cleverly that it curled in wickedly under the bar'.

Passage (k) might present difficulties to a philosopher, though familiar to the specialists who fill in football pools. It is from the *Sunday Express*.

(l) 'Traumatic fractures of the rigid spine of ankylosing spondylitis are reported to unite predictably over a period comparable to those of the normal spine. Conservative measures are sufficient to achieve union and, in the case of cervical spine injuries, the opportunity may even be taken to correct the typical deformaty by a suitably adjustable orthosis. Stress fractures, however, present insidiously at all levels of the spine, though most often at the lower thoracic/lumbar region. The behaviour of the rigid spine when subjected to deforming forces can be compared to that of a long bone, and stress fractures here behave comparably'.

Passage (l) is a typical example of medical language from the *Journal of the Royal Society of Medicine* (Marsh, C. H. Internal fixation for stress fractures of the ankylosed spine. JRSM 1985; 78: 377–379).

(m) 'Slow, slow, slow, with bubble-pause and slide.
He paced before Europa there, and she
As if with shivering drew her shoulders now
Shyly about her, yet she shivered still.
Never did shadow so shimmer with midges
As she with switherings . . .'

Passage (m) is taken from an article in *The Listener*. It illustrates the unusual applications of familiar words and inventions of new ones which are a feature of modern verse.

(n) 'For the consideration aforesaid the Borrowers and Trustees and as Beneficial Owner, hearby charge by way of legal Mortgage ALL THAT the premises described in the First Schedule hereto *with* the payment to the Lender of all the principal money interest and other money payable by the Borrower under the deed *But* subject to the First Mortgage and the term of years Subsisting thereunder and the principal money and interest thereby secured.'

Passage (n) is from a legal document connected with a mortgage. The language is old-fashioned, but such language is still in current use for legal purposes.

(o) 'When the WMA learnt of the constitution and activities of this WHO consultant group it sent delegates to WHO and ILO, first of all to draw attention to the fact that in the WHO consultant group there was no practising doctor, and secondly to put forward its views on social securing schemes in so far as they affect the medical professions in the various countries represented in the WMA.'

Passage (o) is from the first editorial of a highly reputable journal that may be appropriately described as the *BMA*. In the same short article reference is made also to the NHS, APIM, BMA and USA: the second leader introduces us to the HLBP, HRBP and ALBP.

Language, we have seen is a living fabric that is constantly developing, changing as new words come in and others fall by the way. The meanings we attach to words are continually changing too: the changes are often too slow to be evident in a short space of time, but they are clear enough if we look back over a longer period. When a common word is brought into a specialized department, such as that of commerce or sport, it may be used with a specialized meaning that is somewhat different from that which it had originally, and it is easy to see that the meaning of a word may gradually come to be changed in that way. Again, a new discovery or advance may cause a change in viewpoint, and with it a change in the meanings attached to associated words.

The tendency of words to change their meaning by a process of corruption of this kind is one of the most striking facts about language. Many examples of this can be given. The word *presently* used to mean what it says, or *at once*: but generations of procrastinators have corrupted it into its present meaning, *after some time*. *Prevent*, from the Latin *prevenire*, meaning *to come before*, originally meant to *prepare the way* or *assist*: but it has undergone a complete reversal of meaning and now it signifies *hinder*. Other common examples of words that have changed their meanings are *pay, nice, fair, converse, weird, haunt* and *illusion*. Many hundreds of others can be found in the pages of *The Oxford English Dictionary*. There have also been many changes in the pronunciation of words, and this has probably happened in the same way as the changes in meaning. There has been a growth of local or departmental variations, which have gradually spread throughout the whole language. A change of this kind taking place at the present day may be illustrated by the word *either*, in which the pronunciations *eether* and *ither* are both current. Cromwell spelt the word *ayther*, which leaves little doubt about how he pronounced it, and it seems that *ither* is gaining in popularity at the present time. There is rivalry at present between the long and short vowel sounds in *bath, path, glass* etc. The short *a* is still usual in the north of England and in the United States, but the long *ah* sound has now become established in England in the south and west. To anyone brought up in the West Country the long *ah* seems so natural that it comes as a surprise to learn that it is a relatively recent innovation introduced as a fashionable stunt by a set of eighteenth-century beaux, who brought the long Italian *a* back with them after completing their education in Italy. Dr Johnson was very angry about it and wrote a vitriolic protest in the preface to the second edition of his dictionary. There are similar variations in the pronunciation of *new* (often *noo* in the United States), *progress* (long or short *o*) and in the dropping of the *h* from *white* and *whisky* (still pronounced *hwwisky* in Ireland). We are apt to regard the pronunciation we are used to as right and think of the more recent innovations as incorrect: yet here again the only criterion of correctness is usage. As Fowler says, the right thing in pronunciation is to do as our neighbour does.

6

THE LANGUAGE OF THE BUSINESSMAN

Those who move in business circles use a type of language which differs in some respects from that of the scholars, and from the informal language of the home. This may be needed by the businessman who wishes to communicate freely with his English-speaking business associates. The type of language that may be useful is illustrated in the following passages:

1. CAREERS

'The personal attributes which distinguish the successful careers from the rest are many. They vary according to the personality of the individual concerned and the particular career. That said, if I have to choose one common characteristic, it is *commitment*.

There is nothing wrong with a nine-to-five job and every evening spent with the family. Indeed, people with no domestic life are usually incomplete. But, if you want to get to the top in most careers (and again I must stress there is nothing wrong if you do not), then the job has to be a major part of your life.

Perhaps a less pompous way of making the same point is to say that few people make a real success of activities which fail to interest and excite them. So it is crucial to be absolutely sure that the career you choose is the one you really want.'

(Sir Richard Marsh)

2. COOPERATION

'People are not impossible to deal with. Unions are not

impossible to deal with. Bloody-mindedness, if it arises, must do so surely because of misunderstanding. I have not the slightest reservation in making the observation that much of British management doesn't seem to understand the importance of the human factor.'

(Prince Charles)

3. SMALL BUSINESS

'Sir Harold said yesterday that the committee had been impressed by what it had seen of the American Small Business Administration . . . On loan finance, the committee suggests that a publicly underwritten loan guarantee scheme, with a limited subsidy element and some part of the risk retained by the banks, should be set up on an experimental basis as soon as possible.

The argument for a publicly underwritten scheme would become stronger if the case for generally subsidising small firms was accepted. The underwriting of a loan guarantee scheme could prove to be a relatively cost-effective way of making use of whatever resources were available.'

(*The Guardian*)

4. 'The only real security is in earning capacity.'

(Henry Ford)

5. STOCK EXCHANGE

'The lower than expected retail price index and falling money rates gave stock markets a fresh boost yesterday, although turnover slackened. Gilts led the way with gains of one and three-eighths, but an unusual tender 'tap' issue caused some confusion as the market closed.

(*The Guardian*)

6. 'Never ask a servant to do a job that you are not able to do yourself.'

(B Lewis)

7. PHRASES USED IN BUSINESS

We like your new products very much. What discount can you give us on purchases of around £500 if paid for in cash, and what would be your credit terms?

Where are your latest products on display?

I receive only a one per cent commission on sales.

Our goods compete favourably with those of other firms. The rate of exchange is favourable for purchases in our country. We can give a quotation if you wish.

Do you have an agent in New York?

What is the address of the local branch of your firm in London?

Is the cost of delivery included in the price?

Will you please confirm that there are no additional charges. Is this the final invoice?

We would like to keep in touch with you and hear from you about any new developments.

What arrangements have you made for insurance?

7

THE LANGUAGE OF THE SCIENTISTS

English has a special value to the scientist in view of the fact that more scientific books and journals are written in English than in any other language, and the standard of the scientific and technical publications in English is generally high. English is also the language spoken at many international scientific meetings.

More than three centuries ago a group of scientists and philosophers working in England recognized that the everyday language of the ordinary people, and especially that used by poets, although well suited to the expression of feeling and of products of the imagination, was too vague and imprecise for the accurate statement of mathematical principles or scientific laws. They therefore set out to 'improve' the English language by establishing rules of grammar and defining the precise meaning of words. In 1664 the Royal Society appointed a Committee 'for improving the English tongue', and they insisted that when giving lectures and as far as possible at other times their members should use 'a close, naked, natural way of speaking; clear senses; a native easiness, bringing all things as near the mathematical plainness as they can'. As a result of their efforts the English language gained in clarity and precision, so that it became a language that not only poets, but also scientists and philosophers were able to use.

In some scientific and technical publications produced in recent years the standard of the language used is unfortunately not as high as one could wish. Sometimes the excessive use of ill-defined abstract nouns, for example, makes them imprecise and difficult to read. However, the language used in their publications by the leading scientists has nearly always been admirably simple and clear. This is shown by the following examples:

1. 'Absolute, true and mathematical time, of itself, and from its own nature, flows equably without relation to anything external . . .

   Absolute space, in its own nature, without relation to anything external, remains always similar and immovable.'

   (Newton, 1642–1727)

2. 'The main conclusion arrived at in this work, namely that man is descended from some lowly organised form will, I regret to think, be highly distasteful to many. But there can hardly be a doubt that we are descended from barbarians. The astonishment which I felt on first seeing a party of Fuegians on a wild and broken shore will never be forgotten by me, for the reflection at once rushed into my mind – such were our ancestors. These men were absolutely naked and bedaubed with paint, their long hair was tangled, their mouths frothed with excitement, and their expression was wild, startled, and distrustful. They possessed hardly any arts, and like wild animals lived on what they could catch; they had no government, and were merciless to every one not of their own tribe . . . But we are not here concerned with hopes or fears, only with the truth as far as our reason permits us to discover it; and I have given the evidence to the best of my ability. We must, however, acknowledge, as it seems to me, that man with all his noble qualities, with sympathy which feels for the most debased, with benevolence which extends not only to other men but to the humblest living creatures, with his god-like intellect which has penetrated into the movements and constitution of the solar system – with all these exalted powers – Man still bears in his bodily frame the indelible stamp of his lowly origin.'

   (Darwin, 1871)

3. 'The first experiment was made upon a lad of the name of Phipps in whose arm a little vaccine virus was inserted, taken from the hand of a young woman who had been accidentally infected by a cow. Notwithstanding the resemblance which the pustule, thus excited on the boy's arm, bore to variolous inoculation, yet as the indisposition attending it was barely perceptible, I could scarcely persuade myself the patient was secure from the smallpox. However, on his being inoculated some months afterwards, it proved that he was secure . . . At present, I have not the most distant doubt that any person who has once felt the influence of perfect cow pox matter would ever be susceptible to that of the smallpox.'

(Jenner, 1797)

4. 'For the sake of persons of different types of mind, scientific truth should be presented in different forms and should be regarded as equally scientific whether it appears in the robust form and vivid colouring of a physical illustration or in the tenuity and paleness of a symbolic expression.'

(Clerk Maxwell, 1831–1879)

5. 'When you can measure what you are talking about, and express it in numbers, you know something about it; but when you cannot measure it, when you cannot express it in numbers, your knowledge is of a meagre and unsatisfactory kind; it may be the beginning of knowledge, but you have scarcely in your thoughts advanced to the stage of science whatever the matter may be.'

(Lord Kelvin, 1824–1907)

6. 'Early in my career I became convinced that current teaching concerning nutrition was inadequate, and while still a student in hospital in the earlier eighteen-nineties I made up my mind that the part played by nutritional errors in the causation of disease was underrated. The current treatment of

scurvy and rickets seemed to me to ignore the significance of the old recorded observations. I had then a great ambition to study those diseases from a nutritional standpoint, but fate decreed that I was to lose contact with clinical material . . . In 1906–7 I convinced myself by experiments, carried out, as were those of Lunin and Socin, upon mice, that those small animals at any rate could not survive upon a mixture of the basal foodstuffs alone . . . Until the period 1911-12, the earlier suggestions in the literature pointing to the existence of vitamins lay buried . . . Very soon after my chief paper appeared the study of vitamins was, as you know, developed with great energy and success in the United States.'

(Hopkins, 1929)

7. 'One day Geiger came to me and said, 'Don't you think that young Marsden, whom I am training in radioactive methods, ought to begin a small research? Now I had thought that too, so I said, 'Why not let him see if any α-particles can be scattered through a large angle?' I can tell you in confidence that I did not believe they would be . . . Then I remember two or three days later Geiger coming to me in great excitement and saying 'We have been able to get some of the α-particles coming *backwards* . . .' It was quite the most incredible event that has ever happened to me in my life. It was almost as incredible as if you fired a 15-inch shell at a piece of tissue paper and it came back and hit you . . . It was then that I had the idea of an atom with a minute massive centre carrying a charge.'

(Rutherford, 1871–1937)

8. At scientific meetings at which slides are shown there are a few things that the lecturer may need to say to the projectionist, such as: 'The next slide please,' 'Could you focus that slide a little better, please,' and 'Can we have the lights on now, please?'

40

8

THE LANGUAGE OF POETRY

Not everyone likes poetry. Even as distinguished a scholar as Darwin admitted 'I cannot endure to read a line of poetry: I have tried lately to read Shakespeare, and found it so intolerably dull that it nauseated me.' Yet there are many people who get a great deal of pleasure from poetry. It has been said that 'beauty is in the eye of the beholder', and the beauty of poetry can be experienced only by those who have the ability to respond to it and who are willing to give it a trial.

Some English poetry is hard to understand because it uses a special type of language which is different from that of ordinary speech. Sometimes the normal order of the words is changed, and poems often include uncommon words with special associations, which the ordinary reader may not know. Much poetry also uses language of an old-fashioned type, which is no longer in common use. Yet some poetry is written in simple language which differs little from that ordinarily used. Let us look at a few examples:

Leisure

1. What is this life, if full of care,
    We have no time to stand and stare?

    No time to stand beneath the boughs
    And stare as long as sheep or cows:

    No time to see, when woods we pass,
    Where squirrels hide their nuts in grass:

No time to see, in broad daylight,
Streams full of stars, like skies at night:

No time to turn at Beauty's glance,
And watch her feet, how they can dance:

No time to wait till her mouth can
Enrich that smile her eyes began?

A poor life this if, full of care,
We have no time to stand and stare.

(W H Davies)

The Soldier

2.   If I should die, think only this of me:
That there's some corner of a foreign field
That is for ever England. There shall be
In that rich earth a richer dust concealed;
A dust whom England bore, shaped, made aware,
Gave, once, her flowers to love, her ways to roam,
A body of England's, breathing English air.
Wash'd by the rivers, blest by the suns of home . . .

(Rupert Brooke)

Invictus

3.   Out of the night that covers me,
    Black as the pit from pole to pole,
I thank whatever gods may be
    For my unconquerable soul.

In the fell clutch of circumstance
    I have not winced nor cried aloud.
Under the bludgeonings of chance
    My head is bloody, but unbowed.

Beyond this place of wrath and tears
    Looms but the Horror of the shade,
And yet the menace of the years
    Finds and shall find me unafraid.

It matters not how strait the gate,
  How charged with punishment the scroll,
I am the master of my fate:
  I am the captain of my soul.

(W H Henley)

Poetry turns up in many religious services in the form of hymns:

4.   All things bright and beautiful,
      All creatures great and small,
      All things wise and wonderful,
      The Lord God made them all.

      Each little flower that opens,
      Each little bird that sings,
      He made their glowing colours,
      He made their tiny wings.

      The cold wind in the winter,
      The pleasant summer sun,
      The ripe fruits in the garden,
      He made them every one.

(Mrs C F Alexander)

Poetry is not all of a serious kind. There is also a place for light verse:

5.   To the man in the street, who, I'm sorry to say,
      Is a keen observer of life,
      The word 'Intellectual' suggests straightaway
      A man who's untrue to his wife.

(Auden)

6.   Sigh no more, ladies, sigh no more,
      Men were deceivers ever;
      One foot in sea, and one on shore,
      To one thing constant never.

(Shakespeare)

7.   Oh, when I was in love with you,
      Then I was clean and brave,
      And miles around the wonder grew
      How well did I behave.

      And now the fancy passes by,
      And nothing will remain,
      And miles around they'll say that I
      Am quite myself again.

                      (A E Housman)

In the older English poetry and in other kinds of literature we find certain old forms of speech such as the following:

> 'You' is rendered as 'ye', 'thee' or 'thou' followed by an inflected form of the verb.
> 'Your' and 'yours' are rendered as 'thy' and 'thine',
> 'Ever' is rendered as 'e're',
> 'On' is rendered as 'upon'.

If a few differences of this kind are recognized, the language can be understood and the meaning becomes clear, as in the following examples:

8.   'Gather ye rosebuds while ye may,
      Old Time is still a-flying:
      And this same flower that smiles today,
      Tomorrow will be dying.'

                      (Herrick)

9.   'To thine own self be true,
      And it must follow, as the night the day,
      Thou canst not then be false to any man.'

                  (Shakespeare)

The language of poetry uses words and phrases, not only to express thoughts and ideas, but also to arouse feelings and emotions, sometimes of a very moving kind. This is often helped by the use of figures of speech such as meaningful similies and metaphors in which words are given other than their ordinary meanings for the sake of vividness. A metaphor is basically an expression which implies a similarity of one object or situation to another very different one, as in the following examples: *She has a heart of gold. He plowed through the crowd. The ocean of life. All nature smiled.* Another little trick is the bringing together of two or more words beginning with the same letter, which Churchill described as *'alliteration's artful aid.'*

A characteristic feature of most poetry is the use of rhyme, but that is not always the case, as in some of the poems written by the poets of more modern times.

Englishman abroad

10.   The language I have learn'd these forty years,
My native English, now I must forego.
And now my tongue's use is to me no more
Than an unstringed viol or a harp,
Or like a cunning instrument cased up,
Or being open, put into his hands
That knows no touch to tune the harmony.
Within my mouth you have engaoled my tongue,
Doubly portcullised with my teeth and lips;
And dull unfeeling barren ignorance
Is made my gaoler to attend on me.

(Shakespeare)

9

THE COMMON LANGUAGE

Of the several different varieties of English which are used
in different contexts especially important is the Common
Language, which provides a means of communication
between people living in different walks of life, in different
countries and engaged in different fields of work. The
Common Language is used by ordinary people, not only in
their daily lives, but also in learning through the media
about the affairs of the world and in discussing among
themselves all the things that matter to them. How often in
their homes can we hear children asking, 'What do you
mean by that?'. And then their parents are engaged in
trying to explain to them the meaning of a word. In the
schools and colleges the need to understand the meaning of
the language used becomes increasingly important, and
that can present special difficulties for those brought up in
other countries, since many words have different shades of
meaning when translated into other tongues. Even within
the English-speaking regions round the world the range of
different meanings of some words is relatively large, and
that can hinder the free communication and exchange of
ideas. Specially serious are the disagreements which arise
as a result of misunderstandings, which could be avoided if
the precise meanings of the words we use were made more
clear. The definition of words is the purpose of the
dictionaries, many of which are now available, but it would
appear that something more is needed that the curt lists of
definitions which they commonly give. There is a need for
the range of different meanings of many words to be more
fully explained, not in academic terms, but in simple
language of the kind that can be readily understood by all.

There is also a need for relevant information about the changes in meaning which have occurred in some of the words adopted by those engaged in specialist activites such as the sciences and arts.

The words which cause most difficulties are generally abstract terms. Thus the word 'work' is commonly taken to mean 'paid employment', as distinct from unpaid or voluntary work. A person who is unemployed may therefore be said to have no work, although in fact working long hours at housework, gardening or jobs of other kinds. In some contexts the word 'common', which means 'widely available' or 'used by all', is used in a different sense to mean 'inferior', 'undistinguished' or even 'vulgar'.

In the discussion of political matters there are a number of words which can give rise to misunderstandings owing to the range of different meanings they can convey. 'Capitalism' means an economic system based on private enterprise, in which private individuals are free to employ workers to produce the goods and provide the services needed by the community. The word is generally taken to mean a system which maintains individual freedom and human rights, which encourages full employment and which raises the general standard of living by rewarding individual ability. On the other hand 'Capitalism' is understood by some to mean a system which serves the interests of the wealthy by keeping the money in the hands of a few and allowing the rich to exploit the poor.

Another word, 'Democracy', was defined by Abraham Lincoln as 'government of the people by the people for the people': but different meanings can be given to a word which does not state exactly who are 'the people' or how they are to govern. 'Democracy', means basically upholding the interests of the majority of the people rather than those of a privileged few. It can mean a type of social relationship in which all are accepted as equal and accorded equal rights, irrespective of wealth, rank, colour, caste, creed or sex: but the kind of democracy in which a country is governed by the representatives of the people depends very much on the way in which their representatives are elected. In countries such as England, France and the USA there is freedom to nominate representatives, free election by secret ballot, free speech and a free press. However in some other countries which describe themselves as 'Democracies' dissidents opposed to the existing government are not allowed to stand for election, and criticism of the existing government is made a criminal offence. Under those conditions the meaning of 'Democracy' is clearly changed.

Misunderstandings sometimes arise over the meaning of words used in the Courts of Law. Thus there have been protests in the press over the relatively light sentences sometimes passed against individuals convicted of murder, and it has been urged that for a crime of such severity the sentences should be uniformly severe. Yet what exactly do we mean by 'Murder'? Certainly there are cases where one person brutally attacks and kills another, and in such cases the sentence should certainly be severe: but that is not always the way in which things happen. At the other extreme are the cases in which the killing is little more than an unintended accident or an act of self-defence. A similar wide range of different meanings can also apply to other legal terms such as 'Abuse', 'Libel' and 'Rape'. Even the word 'Marriage' has a special meaning for those who have grown up in Indian communities in which marriage is largely regarded as primarily a family affair requiring the provision of a substantial dowry by the family of the bride.

Another word which gives rise to misunderstandings is 'Life', which is commonly associated with the conscious experience of actively pursuing aims, exercising skills, having adventures, loving and enjoying the fulfilment of desires. Life is regarded by many as our most precious possession, and it is therefore hardly surprising that there is strong opposition to scientists engaging in embryo research, which destroys life. However it is not always appreciated that an embryo is little more than a bundle of cells, with neither a brain nor a heart, so that 'Life' in an embryo is something very different from that in a fully developed human being, or even in a new-born child. The Common Language certainly provides an excellent means of communication which is widely used in many different countries, but clearly it is important for those who use it to appreciate the wide range of meanings of many ordinary words, and sometimes to clarify the precise meaning in which a word is used.

Difficulties of communication sometimes arise through the use of expressions known as idioms, which are commonly used in most regions but not always known in all. An idiom is a verbal expression with a meaning which is different from that logically expressed by the words used in it. Thus a person who is healthy may be said to be *fit as a fiddle*, while one who is thin may be described as *thin as a rake*, and one who is intelligent is *highbrow*. There are many well-known expressions of this kind, such as: *Once in a blue moon. A square peg in a round hole. Like a red rag to a bull.* Confusing to visitors from other countries are also the multiple meanings of some words, e.g. *What really counts is what cannot be counted.* The wide range of different meanings of some common English words is illustrated by those included in the following section, which contains also a number of technical terms of the kind that are commonly used at scientific and other international meetings.

10

DIFFERENT MEANINGS OF WORDS

A number of well-known English words have a range of different meanings which are not always known to those who use them, and that is often the reason for the difficulties of communication and misunderstandings that arise. That applies especially to Common Language words which have special meanings in the Courts of Law or in scientific, religious or other different contexts. Personal difficulties can also be caused by the misinterpretation of medical terms. The words included in this section are selected as examples of those which cause problems of different kinds.

☆   ☆   ☆

ABILITY
ABSTRACT
ADDICTION
AGGRESSION
ALCOHOLISM
ALLERGY
ANTIBIOTIC
ANXIETY
ARGUMENT
AUTISM

BEAUTY
BEHAVIOURISM
BLASPHEMY

CAPITALISM
CAUSE
CELEBRATION
CHARITY
COMA
COMMUNICATION
COMMUNISM
CONFABULATION
CONFESSION
CONGENITAL
CONSCIENCE
CONTRACT
CONTROL
CRUELTY

DEATH
DEFAMATION
DELUSION
DEMOCRACY
DEPRESSION
DIAGNOSIS
DISEASE
DOGMA
DRUG

ENERGY
EPILEPSY
ESTABLISHMENT
EVIDENCE
EXISTENTIALISM
EXPLANATION

FAITH
FIXTURE
FREQUENCY
FRUSTRATION
FUNCTION

GENETIC
GOD
GOOD
GOVERNMENT
GUARANTEE

HEALTH
HUMANISM
HUMOUR
HYSTERIA

IMMUNITY
IMPOTENCE
INFLATION
INFORMATION
INSIGHT
INTELLIGENCE

LIFE
LIGHT
LOVE
LUCK

MARRIAGE
MATERIALISM
MEMORY
MENTAL DISORDER
MIRACLE

NEGLIGENCE

OBESITY
OBSCENITY
OBSESSION

PACIFISM
PAIN
PEACE
PERIOD
PERSONALITY
PHILOSOPHY
PHOBIA
PHYSIOLOGY
PIRACY
PLANT
PRAGMATIC
PREVALENCE
PROVOCATION
PSYCHIATRY

RATIONAL
REALISM
REALITY
REHABILITATION
RELIGION
REMUNERATION

SANCTION
SCIENCE
SENSE
SHOCK
SOVEREIGNTY
SPIRITUALISM
STRESS
STRUCTURE
SUICIDE

TECHNOLOGY
THEOLOGY
TRIBUNAL

UNCONSCIOUS
UNDERWRITING
UNIVERSAL

VALUE
VANDALISM
VECTOR
VEGETARIAN
VIOLENCE
VIVISECTION

WILL
WISDOM
WORK

☆   ☆   ☆

ABILITY

Common language

Ability is the proficiency in performing a task requiring
physical or mental skill. *Specific abilities* include those of
academic, artistic, athletic, musical, professional and other
kinds. *General ability* is a loose expression meaning the
ability to cope with a wide range of problems of different
types. Abilities are dual in nature, since they depend on a
combination of (a) innate capabilities and (b) practical
skills acquired by training and practice in an environment
suitable for their development. The extent to which
hereditary qualities and acquired skills contribute to ability
varies widely in different individuals and in abilities of
different types. Thus one person may be a 'born performer'
while another acquires a similar degree of ability only after
long training and many failures. Some abilities, such as
reading and writing, can be acquired by anyone of average
intelligence who is suitably taught, but high mathematical
or creative artistic abilities can be developed only in
specially gifted individuals with innate qualities that are
relatively rare. A person may have a number of diverse
abilities, being relatively strong in some and weak in others.

Psychology
Mental ability has been held to be made up of a number of *primary mental abilities* (PMA) or different traits. Seven unit traits derived by factor analysis are *verbal comprehension* (V), *word fluency* (W) *number* (N), *space* (S), *associative memory* (M), *perceptual speed* (P) and *reasoning* (R) or *induction* (I).

ABSTRACT

Common language
As an adjective, the word 'abstract' is applied to any principle, idea or concept abstracted by processes of thought from factual evidence or concrete material. Thus, the abstract concept 'kindness' is derived by a process of generalization from the behaviour of persons who are kind.

Law
1. An abstract is a short analysis of a legal document. For example, an *Abstract of Title* is a short analysis of a document establishing the right of ownership to a particular estate.

Art
2. An abstract is a work of art which excludes any reference to reality existing outside it. In other words, it contains no forms that can be directly identified as belonging to the real world. The word 'abstract' is commonly used in this sense in Europe.
3. The word 'abstract' is used also in another sense for any work of art which is *significantly withdrawn* from the direct representation of visual reality. It may thus contain figurative representations of real forms so long as the work as a whole is not intended as a supposedly direct transcription of vision. The word 'abstract' is commonly used in this sense in the United States.

Science
4. An abstract is a brief noncritical statement of the essentials contained in a particular piece of published or reported material.
5. An abstract is a passage reproduced word for word from published or reported material.

ADDICTION

Common language

1. Addiction is a state of involuntary continuation of a bad habit such as the excessive drinking of alcohol or taking drugs, which the addict is unable to stop.
(See ALCOHOLISM.)

Medicine

2. Addiction is a pathological state resulting from repeated administration of a drug, in which a characteristic illness (withdrawal symptoms) occurs if supplies of the drug are withdrawn. The severity of the withdrawal symptoms is such that the addict finds it difficult or impossible to stop taking the drug: the compulsive craving can cause a disorganization of the personality which may result in antisocial or criminal behaviour.

Addiction differs from drug *habituation*, in which drug-taking is established as a habit, but serious withdrawal symptoms are not experienced and voluntary cessation of the habit is possible. Addiction and habituation are different forms of *drug dependence*: the characteristics of drug dependence vary according to the nature of the drug concerned. Special types of drug dependence have been defined by the World Health Organization Expert Committee on Addiction Producing Drugs (WHO tech. Rep. Ser. 1964, *273*, 1): for example drug dependence of barbiturate type, of morphine type, of amphetamine type, etc. Terms such as *morphinism* and *alcoholism* have been used to describe particular forms of addiction; but various different meanings have been given to these terms. The term *drug abuse* is comonly used for drug addiction in the United States of America; but this term implies also an attitude of moral judgement.

AGGRESSION

Common Language. (1) Aggression is an unprovoked attack or threat of attack. The meaning of the word is sometimes extended to include (2) antisocial behaviour such as damaging or taking away another person's possessions, or (3) any invasion of 'rights', as by restricting or threatening to restrict another person's freedom. While the word is used to describe certain kinds of *behaviour*, it is used also in another sense for a *personality trait* which is described also as 'aggressiveness'. In this sense (4) aggression is the tendency or inclination to attack other people, or (5) to force one's own views or interests on other people.

Biology (6) Aggression is the tendency to seek dominance in a social group, or (7) aggression is behaviour that induces fear or flight in another animal. Herbert Spencer regarded aggression as an instinct, and this view has been accepted by some biologists such as Lorenz, who has described aggression as (8) 'the fighting instinct in beast and man which is directed against members of the same species'. Other biologists do not accept the view that aggression is an instinct or that it is directed only towards members of the same species.

Psychology. Psychologists have used the word in sense (1) of the common language for an attack on another person; but the meaning has sometimes been restricted to an attack in response to opposition, and some psychologists have defined aggression as (9) any behavioural response to frustration. Adler regarded aggression as (10) a manifestation of the will to power, in contrast to 'social feeling', which is recognition of the needs of others. Freud and other analysts have regarded aggression as (11) a form of 'destructive energy' which is a projection of a 'death instinct' (hate): it may be contrasted with the 'life instinct' (love). In this sense aggression may lead to self-destruction as well as to destruction of others.

ALCOHOLISM

Medicine
Alcoholism is a term that has been used to describe a number of different conditions associated with excessive consumption of alcohol. It is not easy to draw a sharp distinction between these conditions, since one may develop gradually into another.

The regular or occasional *heavy drinker*, who drinks for pleasure, may be distinguished from the chronic *habitué* or *drunkard*, in whom excessive drinking is established as a habit. The word *alcoholic* is generally reserved for a compulsive drinker who is (a) unable to abstain from the habit or (b) unable to stop drinking when once he has started: he is therefore alcohol dependent, or an addict. The drinking of the *habitué* may depend to a large extent on the circumstances and he may change his habits if the circumstances are changed: but the dependence of the *alcoholic* on alcohol is affected relatively little by external circumstances and requires more radical treatment if it is to be changed. An *alcoholic psychotic* is a person suffering from a form of mental illness due to brain damage resulting from excessive drinking of alcohol with associated vitamin deficiencies. There are a number of different forms of alcoholic psychosis. Acute forms include *alcoholic delirium (delirium tremens* or *DTs)* in which hallucinations are often a prominent symptom. Chronic forms of alcoholic psychosis include *Korsakow's syndrome*, which is characterized especially by loss of memory for recent events, with compensatory confabulation.

(See ADDICTION.)

Excessive drinking may be either a cause or a symptom of illness. The following different forms of alcoholism may be distinguished:

(1) Excessive drinking is a symptom of an underlying personality disorder. The sufferer may turn to alcohol for relief from feelings of anxiety, depression or insecurity.

(2) Excessive drinking is mainly a consequence of the drinking customs in the drinker's culture or group. This is seen for example in certain clubs and business circles where alcoholic entertainment is the rule.

(3) Some individuals are able to abstain for long periods, but once started, despite good intentions, they lose control and end up drunk. Often the first drink is decisive.

(4) Alcoholism may take the form of constant daily tippling, without often getting drunk. The drinker does not lose control and can stop drinking in good time on any special occasion, but the regular excessive drinking, combined with bad dietary habits, undermines a person's

general health and working efficiency. This pattern of alcoholic addiction is especially common in the wine-drinking countries.

(5) Alcoholism may take the form of periodic drinking bouts or 'sprees'. As in other forms of alcoholism, this may lead to loss of working efficiency, disturbance of family and social life and deterioration of the drinker's physical and mental health.

(6) A World Health Organisation committee in 1951 adopted the definition: 'Alcoholics are those excessive drinkers whose dependence on alcohol has attained such a degree that it shows a noticeable mental disturbance or an interference with their bodily and mental health, their interpersonal relations and their smooth social and economic functioning; or those who show the prodromal signs of such development.'

ALLERGY

Pathology

1. Derived from the Greek words meaning 'altered reactivity', the word *allergy* was introduced by Burke (1906) to describe an abnormal sensitivity to a specific foreign substance, which he observed in certain pathological conditions. Allergy implies a response of certain tissues of the body to quantities of a specific chemical substance to which in most members of the same species there is no response. Allergy is of two broad types (a) *immediate*, or acting in a matter of seconds, as in hay-fever or nettle-rash (urticaria), and (b) *delayed*, or requiring several hours and reaching a maximum response after one or two days, as in contact dermatitis. The use of the word is now generally restricted to conditions in which there is hypersensitivity attributable to an antigen-antibody reaction; but formerly some investigators included increased sensitivity due to any cause, and also reduced sensitivity, as manifestations of allergy. Among the substances liable to produce an allergic reaction are plant pollens, bacterial toxins, foreign proteins, feathers, fur, plastics, ingredients in soaps and cosmetics, penicillin and many drugs. Allergy to a specific

substance can be demonstrated in some cases by a skin test, in which the substance is applied to the skin and the local reaction is observed: but an allergic reaction may be limited to one organ and it is not necessarily shown by the skin. It is believed that an allergic reaction of the bronchi plays an important part in asthma, and that similarly there is an allergic hyper-sensitivity of the naso-pharynx in hay fever and allergic rhinitis. Allergy is also believed to play a part in serum sickness, collagen disease, coeliac disease, tropical sprue, angioneurotic oedema, anaphylaxis, cold allergy, migraine, and in certain forms of eczema.

Common Language
2. The word has now come into the Common Language where it is used loosely to imply an abnormal sensitivity in personal relations (antipathy) towards some specific type of individual: e.g. *allergic to cats, to prima-donnas, to politicians, et al.*

ANTIBIOTIC

Biology
1. A chemical substance which acts selectively in destroying or restricting the growth of one or more living organisms. This includes fungicides and insecticides used to control insect pests, as well as disinfectants and the chemotherapeutic agents used to combat bacterial, protozoal and viral infections in veterinary work and in medicine.

There are two large classes of antibacterial compounds (a) *bactericides*, which kill bacteria when administered at a suitable concentration, and (b) *bacteriostats*, which do not kill bacteria directly, but prevent their multiplication. Some antibiotics act on bacteria by altering the structure of the cell-wall; others act by interfering with the assimilation or utilization of energy-supplying nutrients. Pencillin is believed to act on staphylococci by inhibiting the uptake of glutamic acid, so that they are unable to synthesise the proteins needed for growth. Streptomycin appears to act by interfering with the utilization of pyruvate as a source of energy.

Medicine

2. The word 'antibiotic' is also used in a more restricted sense for a chemical substance that acts selectively in destroying or restricting the growth of micro-organisms in the tissues of a living animal. Antibiotics are thus distinguished from antiseptics, which are generally too toxic to be administered to an animal in doses that would be effective against micro-organisms in the living tissues of the body.

ANXIETY

Common Language

Anxiety is (1) an emotional state charactertized by feelings of apprehension or inadequacy, which can be induced by a vague threat or possible risk, as when an important decision has to be made. It may be associated with a sense of inadequacy, real or imagined, to deal with a difficulty which may arise. In *acute anxiety*, which is an immediate response to a situation of stress, the onset is abrupt and sometimes marked by an unnatural tone of voice and feelings of choking or suffocation 'a lump in the throat'. There may be physical signs of anxiety such as sweating, palpitations, tremors, and urinary frequency, with loss of appetite, sleeplessness, headache and a feeling of fatigue. An anxious person may be overactive, or impulsiveness may be restricted by dread of the consequences of action, so that action is inhibited. There is an inability to concentrate or to take part normally in the affairs of life. In *chronic anxiety* the symptoms are milder and more poorly defined, but feelings of restlessness and tension, with an inability to relax, can continue for a considerable time.

Anxiety is a normal reaction in situations of stress, as for example when severe competition imposes a threat to a person's status or career; but when anxiety is excessive, or when it persists without due cause, it is then pathological and constitutes a form of neurosis. An *anxiety neurosis* can occur as a result of conscious or unconscious mental conflict, as when a person's desires or behaviour come into conflict with their conscience.

Anxiety can also mean (2) concern or solicitude, as when a person is 'anxious to help'.

ARGUMENT

Common Language

1. An argument is a statement intended to influence the mind in accepting or rejecting a proposal, assertion or proposition: it is a statement of reasons or evidence for or against a view in a discussion or debate.

Arguments may vary in the extent to which they are convincing, compelling or strong (cogent). They vary also in kind. An argument which is not logically sound is a *fallacy*, and the deliberate use of fallacious arguments is known as *sophistry*. An argument may be fallacious in that

(a) it misstates the facts (misrepresentation).
(b) it uses incorrect reasoning (e.g. a *non sequitur*), or
(c) it contains words that are wrongly used.

To be accepted as sound, an argument must be logically correct (or free from fallacies) and also impersonal and objective in character, so as to exclude personal bias or prejudice. Of the many different kinds of fallacies and tricks of argument that are recognized, the following may be noted:

(a) *Arguing in a circle*. (E.g. 'The rightness of his policy shows that Smith is a great statesman. Because Smith is a great statesman, his policy must be right.')

(b) *Begging the question*, or a *false syllogism*. Drawing a conclusion from a basis that also needs to be proved. (E.g. 'The woman must be a witch because she keeps a black cat, and women who keep black cats are well known to be witches.')

(c) *Irrelevant conclusion*. Proving something different from the point in question (e.g. If the real question is whether it is legal to park a car in a certain place, proving instead that it *ought* to be legal to do so).

(d) *The 'red herring'*. This is a particular case of the fallacy

60

of irrelevant conclusion, in which an irrelevant argument is introduced, or a side-issue is developed, to distract attention from the main question at issue.

(e) *Non sequitur ('it does not follow')*. The fallacy of assuming a causal relationship on inadequate evidence. (E.g. 'Buzzards have been seen feeding on dead lambs: they are therefore destructive to livestock.' The argument would be valid only if it were proved that the buzzards killed the lambs).

(f) *The 'post hoc' fallacy*. This is the common fallacy of assuming that an event *preceding* a particular occurrence must be the *cause* of it: it is a particular case of *non sequitur* (e.g. 'He took the doctor's medicine on Monday and died the very next day: therefore the medicine caused his death'.)

(g) *The 'feminine argument'* (Schopenhauer). The opponent's argument is misrepresented by exaggerating it. (E.g. 'You say that we should economize? You mean you cannot afford to keep me!')

(h) *Faulty generalization*. Applying to all the members of a group what is really applicable to a few. (E.g. 'The Germans are guilty of the murders at Belsen: therefore every German is cruel') or because the children of large families are less intelligent *on the average* than children of small families, it is argued that *every* child of a large family must be unintelligent.

(i) *Confusion of fact and hypothesis*. An unproven hypothesis is represented as an established fact.

(j) *False antithesis*. A contrast is used for the purpose of misrepresentation. (E.g. As when a speaker contrasts the purity of his own motives with the baseness of the motives he attributes to his opponent.)

(k) *Equivocation*. Using a term in two different senses at different stages in a train of reasoning. (E.g. 'Every sunset is a miracle: what greater proof is needed of the truth of the miracles of Our Lord?')

(l) *False analogy (erroneous correspondence)*. If two things have *one* attribute in common, it is assumed that *another* attribute must also be shared by both. (E.g. Because Smith dresses well and is wealthy, it is argued that Jones, who dresses well, must also be wealthy.)

(m) *Undistributed middle*. This is the fallacy of regarding a statement of limited applicability as universally true. (E.g.

Henry VIII was a virile man. Mary likes virile men. Therefore Mary must like Henry VIII.' The conclusion is true only if Mary's liking for virile men, expressed in the middle statement (of the syllogism), applies to *all* virile men, or is 'universally distributed'.)

(n) *'Loaded' arguments.* These are arguments calculated to persuade by exploiting the sentiments, prejudices, etc. of the individual addressed. Thus, by appealing to a person's professed patriotism or by relying on his ignorance, modesty, greed, or fears, an argument may be more persuasive than it would be to an impartial person. (E.g. 'No true American would listen to . . .' 'If you had read the works of Smith, you would know . . .' 'Einstein was not of your opinion: but perhaps you know better.')

(o) *Introducing personalities.* A known personality, such as the hearer himself or a member of his family, is discussed, so that the question at issue cannot be judged impartially.

(p) Personal abuse and the threat of force are not arguments, but an admission of defeat in argument, since the speaker is resorting to persuasion by other means.

2. An argument is a controversy, contention or exchange of views between two or more persons holding different opinions, each trying to refute the other's views. An argument in which hostile feelings are expressed may be described as a dispute, wrangling or a quarrel. An argument differs from a *debate*, which must be conducted according to recognized rules. An argument may be contrasted with a *discussion*, in which the primary aim is the careful consideration of evidence and the reconciliation of any differences of opinion.

3. Argument is the act of debating, contending, arguing, or stating the pros and cons of an assertion.

Logic

4. An argument is a statement of reasoning expressed in words.

5. An argument stated in its regular form is a *syllogism*. From the premises laid down as granted, a conclusion or inference is deduced, i.e. it must be admitted to be true as necessarily resulting from the premises.

Literature
6. The argument of a book or other literary work is a short statement of the subject-matter or story.

Mathematics
7. The argument is a value given to an independent variable in an equation that determines a specific value for a dependent variable.
8. The argument is a value used to extract a related value, the *consequent*, from a table.

AUTISM

Psychiatry
The word has been used loosely to describe a type of thinking, a personality trait, a symptom or a pathological condition.
1. A tendency towards a self-centred type of thinking dominated by subjective material and showing little concern for objective reality.
2. Preoccupation with wish-fulfilling fantasies (as in 'day-dreaming'.)
3. A behavioural syndrome characterized by inability to form emotional relationships with other people and consequent withdrawal into an inner life detached from external reality.
Kanner (1943) described *early infantile autism* (Kanner's Syndrome) as a psychiatric syndrome appearing generally after the first few months of life and characterized especially by unresponsiveness when picked up and nursed: the baby wants to be left alone and will not be cuddled. He may be abnormally quiet or he may scream for long periods for no apparent reason, and he may not accept a normal routine of feeding and sleeping. Speech is retarded and often characterized by the senseless repetition of words or phrases heard (echolalia); the child is slow to use language as a means of communication. Autistic children are generally good-looking and they look intelligent, but they tend to be absorbed in their own individual interests and unresponsive to external

63

influences. In many cases there is an intellectual defect and evidence of brain damage. The basic disability appears to be a special difficulty in the meaningful interpretation of auditory and visual data.

The term *'autistic'* is sometimes applied loosely to a child who will not play with other children or who shows some of the other features of Kanner's Syndrome. The belief, which was held at one time, that childhood autism is a form of schizophrenia, is no longer held by most authorities: autistic children may in time achieve a partial adjustment to their disability, but they do not generally develop into schizophrenics in later life.

BEAUTY

Common Language
Beauty is (1) the quality of anything which gives feelings of pleasure or gratification at a high aesthetic, cultural or intellectual level. Besides the beauties of nature, such as beautiful scenery and sunsets, beauty may be found in the form and features of a human face, in the colours and design of a painting, or in the rhythm and harmony of a musical composition. 'Beauty is the one form of spirituality we experience through the senses' (Plato): but beauty can be appreciated best by those who have the necessary cultural and intellectual backgrounds 'beauty is in the eye of the beholder'. One person may see beauty in a desert, while another sees there only ugliness.

Beauty is also used in a concrete sense for (2) a beautiful person or thing, such as a beautiful woman or a beautiful babe.

Technology
Beauty is (3) the fitness for purpose of a piece of equipment 'beauty in engineering is that which has no superfluous parts and exactly suits its purpose' (Ferguson).

Philosophy
Authorities differ widely in their judgements as to which things are beautiful and in what they mean by 'beauty'.

Beauty has been attributed variously to qualities such as (a) that which gives pleasure, (b) that which excites emotions, (c) that which induces a specific emotion, (d) that which reveals truth, (e) that which reveals the spirit of nature, (f) that which is an achievement of genius, (g) that which heightens vitality, (h) that which points to perfection, and (i) that which reveals an ideal. The word 'beauty' can thus have many different meanings.

BEHAVIOURISM

Common Language
Behaviourism is (1) the materialistic attitude or belief that people's behaviour is determined largely by the mechanical operation of neurological mechanisms in the brain, rather than by their conscious feelings and personal desires.

Psychology
Behaviourism is (2) a doctrine based on the systematic observation of human and animal behaviour in responding to stimuli. It maintains that behaviour is a mechanical response to internal and environmental stimuli, which can account for all psychological phenomena and that factors such as mind, intellect, consciousness and introspection should be regarded as irrelevant. It emphasises a machine-like quality in human and animal behaviour.

BLASPHEMY

Common Language
1. Outrageously irreverent speaking about God or about anything held sacred.

Law
2. In the sixth century the Emperor Justinian imposed penalties for blasphemy on the grounds that it endangered the public safety by provoking the anger of God. Later rulers held that in attacking the established religion blasphemy constituted an attack on the state. The

nineteenth-century Courts acted on the principle that defamation of the fundamental truths of Christianity is provocative of disorder and could cause a breach of the peace. In 1922 Mr Justice Avory defined the offence of blasphemy as 'indecent and offensive attacks on Christianity or the scriptures, or sacred places or objects, calculated to outrage the feelings of the general body of the community'.

CAPITALISM

Common Language
Capitalism is (1) an economic system based on private enterprise, in which private individuals and companies are free to use the capital they possess to develop and run workshops, factories, farms and other institutions employing paid workers who produce goods and provide the services which are wanted by the community. The capital system emphasises the value of money, since production is stimulated by the profits obtained, there is free competition and the quantity of goods produced is determined by the cost of production and the price at which they can be sold.

Sociology
Capitalism has been criticised by some who regard it as (2) a system serving the interests of capitalists rather than those of the community. It perpetuates social inequality by keeping the wealth (capital) in the hands of a few and allowing the rich to exploit the poor. It is a system in which the main motive is private profit and in which people pursue their own interests regardless of the interests of the community. In contrast to the socialist principle 'to every man according to his needs' it maintains the principle 'to every man according to what he can pay'.

On the other hand others support capitalism as (3) a system consistent with individual freedom and human rights, in which any disadvantages can be controlled by law. It is a system which encourages full employment and which in many countries has raised the general standard of living by keeping prices low and by rewarding individual ability, initiative, industry and thrift. It is a system with many advantages as well as limitations.

CAUSE

Common Language
1. That which brings about an effect.
2. That which is responsible, in part or in whole, for an event. Causes are of several different kinds: an object, a person, a purpose, a motive, an event, a set of circumstances or an 'act of God' can be regarded as a cause.

Science
3. Any factor established as contributing to the occurrence of a given event. Often a number of different factors interact in leading to an event and we cannot accept any one factor as the sole cause: it may not be easy to assess their relative importance or to determine whether an associated factor is causally related or not. Thus an accident may result from a combination of bad design, mechanical failure, negligence and poor judgement, any of which may be considered to be a cause.
4. A sufficient condition that must precede if a given change is to occur: a sufficient condition to bring about a given change in later behaviour. The fact that a condition is associated with and precedes a given change does not show that it is necessarily the cause. Only if it is established that the condition *invariably* precedes a given change can the induction be made that the condition is the cause.

Philosophy
5. Plato distinguished two kinds of causes: those which produce effects through the operation of a rational purpose (as when motivated by love), and those which produce chance effects in a chaotic way not subject to laws. Aristotle recognized four kinds of causes (a) *material causes*, such as earth and water, (b) *formal causes*, which are in the essential nature of material objects, (c) *efficient causes*, which are motions or changes and (d) *final causes*, in which the cause is

a purpose directed towards a final end. Since all changes must have an ultimate origin, he described a *First Cause*, or the 'unmoved mover', which started all subsequent movement at the beginning of time. Hume challenged the assumption that there is ever any necessary connexion between cause and effect. He maintained that the belief that they are related is an inference drawn from our experience that the one frequently follows the other; and he concluded that there is nothing in cause except invariable succession. Kant rejected this view and regarded the relation of cause and effect as a basic concept reflecting the constitution of the human mind.

Law
6. The evidence, arguments and pleas put forward by one side in a law-suit or in a dispute: *to plead one's cause*.

CELEBRATION

Common Language
1. Festivities or public ceremonies held as an expression of thankfulness over a happy event.
2. An indulgence or other observance serving to commemorate an event such as a marriage, or a birthday.

Theology
3. A formal procedure used to give symbolic expression to convictions or beliefs, as in the solemnization of the Eucharist and the performance of other religious rites and ceremonies.

CHARITY. CHARITABLE

Common Language
1. The early meaning of the word charity was Christian love towards our fellow men. This meaning still survives in some contexts and it is evident in the adjective *charitable*, which generally means an attitude which is kind, considerate, generous and tolerant of the weakness of others, as in one

who is inclined to judge favourably the motives and actions of other people. Charity is essentially disinterested, and not seeking a return. As it was put by St Paul:

> 'Charity suffereth long and is kind; charity envieth not; charity vaunteth not itself, is not puffed up, doth not behave itself unseemly, seeketh not her own, is not easily provoked, thinketh not evil; rejoiceth not in iniquity, but rejoices in the truth; beareth all things, believeth all things, hopeth all things, endureth all things.'

While charity was acclaimed as a virtue, the meaning attached to the word was influenced by the teaching of the churches which urged that the wealthy should give money to the poor, since in that way they could remove their sin. With the development of charitable institutions designed for this purpose, charity became for many people a social duty rather than a form of love for all. Some even took the trouble to enquire into the morals of those in need so that charitable help could be given only to the 'deserving poor'. Under these conditions the acceptance of charity came to be regarded as degrading by the recipients, who felt that to take charity was damaging to their dignity and self-respect.

In the modern welfare state the situation has changed and the provision of welfare benefits for the poor has come to be regarded by them, not as a charity, but as a right.

2. The word 'charity' is now commonly used in a different sense for the public institutions registered by the Charity Commission for carrying out voluntary activities of different kinds. While most of these bodies, such as those involved with medical care or famine relief, are efficiently run and doing excellent work, the purpose and efficiency of others have been questioned, and this has come to affect the meaning of the word 'charity' used in this sense.

Law

In the United Kingdom legal recognition is restricted to charities of four types which are designed for (1) the relief of poverty, (2) the advancement of education, (3) the advancement of religion, and (4) other purposes beneficial to the community (excluding the other three). An organisation wishing to be registered as a charity must come within one of these four categories, and their precise definition has frequently given rise to legal problems. Registered charities enjoy considerable financial advantages in the form of tax relief and many voluntary organisations have therefore sought recognition as a charity, but this has generally been refused to organisations which might participate in political activities or whose benefit to the community might be questioned.

COMA

Medicine
1. Coma is a state of complete unconsciousness in which purposive responses to stimuli are absent, but reflex activity is present and there may be unspecific generalised responses to powerful stimuli such as pain. In other words, there is no evidence of activity at a cortical level, but the lower centres of the brain remain active. Coma is said to be deep or light, according to the degree. The degree of coma at any time may be defined by stating which reflex activities are present and which are not (e.g. responsiveness to principles or obstruction of breathing, corneal and pupillary reflexes, plantar responses, swallowing reflex and tendon jerks.
2. Some authorities define coma at a deeper level, as a state of unconsciousness in which both purposive and reflex activity are absent, and the functions of the body are practically limited to circulation and respiration (Warren).
3. Coma is defined by the Brain Injuries Committee of the Medical Research Council (1941) as:

> 'A state of absolute unconsciousness, as judged by the absence of any psychologically understandable response (including, for example, change of expression) to external stimuli or inner need.'

They note: 'It is not uncommon to hear it said by a patient who is comatose and cannot swallow that he is 'deeply unconscious'. This statement has no real value. He should be said to be comatose with loss of swallowing reflex'.

Light coma, or *semicoma*, is defined as: 'A state in which psychologically understandable responses are elicited only by painful or other disagreeable stimuli, e.g. pinching the skin, or shaking the patient vigorously.

Coma occurs in a great many pathological conditions in which the function of the brain is impaired. This may occur through tissue damage, through the action of drugs, or through the lack of the blood constituents required for the normal activity of the brain. Different types of coma commonly recognized include uremic coma, diabetic coma, hypoglycaemic coma, hepatic coma, pituitary coma and alcoholic coma. Coma may also be caused by cerebral haemorrhage, narcotic poisoning, carbon monoxide, head injury and infective conditions, such as malaria. Coma is associated with a considerable decrease (30–50%) in the circulation and oxygen consumption of the brain, and generally with the absence of electrical activity of the cerebral cortex, as indicated by the electroencephalograph.

COMMUNICATION

Common Language
1. One meaning of communication is the joining or sharing of the community, as in participation in Holy Communion. This meaning of the word also occurs in terms such as *lines of communication* established by roads, railways and canals, which enable individuals to join the communities living in other regions of the land.
2. A more usual meaning of the word is the transfer of information or ideas from one individual to another. Communication may be by sight or by sound, but other senses may also be involved, and in many mammalian species a part is played by the secretion of pheromones which convey information by the sense of smell.

COMMUNISM

Common Language
Communism is (1) a doctrine of extreme revolutionary

socialism which maintains that the working-class must take over power from the capitalist class, if necessary by the use of force, so that all means of production become publicly owned and the private ownership of workshops, factories, land etc. must be abolished. Society must then be reorganised in the interests of the majority of the people in accordance with the principles as expressed by Karl Marx: 'From every man according to his ability, to every man according to his needs.' Certain principles of communism described by Marx and developed by Engels are known as 'Dialectical materialism'.

The term 'communism' is applied not only to the teachings of communists such as Karl Marx but also to (2) the associated social and political movements and more specifically to (3) the systems of government established in the USSR and other communist countries. Communist teachings and governments have taken several different forms in different countries and have changed to some extent in the years since the Russian revolution of 1917.

Sociology
The meaning of communism varies widely in different sections of the community. Some regard the forms of communist government developed in Soviet countries as (4) dictatorships running beaurocracies which have delayed human progress and deprived citizens of their just freedoms and human rights. Others regard them as (5) systems which have succeeded in ending the previous class distinctions and exploitations of the workers by the wealthy.

CONFABULATION

Common Language
1. An informal chat.

Psychiatry
2. Confabulation is the fabrication of false recollections of past or recent events. It commonly occurs for example as a symptom in alcoholic and senile psychoses. A patient may relate with conviction events which never took place and

give variable accounts – each version believed by the patient at the time – to fill in gaps of memory caused by brain damage. The retrospective falsification may consist in the adding of false details or giving a false interpretation or colouring to a true memory of events that did happen. In organic brain disorders the false memories are sometimes of a fantastic or extravagant kind and in the nature of delusional beliefs: but confabulation of a milder kind is not uncommon in persons regarded as normal, when recollections of past events are unconsciously modified by emotional bias or by an attempt to rationalize or conventionalize in adapting the memories to the cultural background of the individual.

Pathological lying (pseudologia fantastica) differs from confabulation in that there is a more or less deliberate attempt to deceive. But untrue statements sometimes come to be believed by those who make them and then it may be hard to draw a sharp distinction between pathological lying and confabulation.

3. In mental testing by the Rorschach Inkblot method the term 'confabulation' is used in a special sense for the category of unorganized, rambling responses of a subject carried away by illogical thinking.

CONFESSION

Common Language
1. A confession is a voluntary statement admitting a belief or an attitude of mind, e.g. a confession of faith, or a declaration of sympathy for a cause.
2. A confession is a voluntary admission of weakness, fault, guilt, or responsibility, in part or in whole, for an act that contravenes a particular criminal, civil, military, moral or religious code.

Law
3. A confession is the voluntary acknowledgement before the proper authority of the truth of a charge.
4. A confession is a statement made by an accused, in which the words of admission in their context expressly or substantially admit guilt, or if the words were taken

together in their context inferentially admit guilt. According to Lord Guest in Anandagoa v The Queen (1962), in judging whether a particular statement is a confession, it is irrelevant to consider whether the accused *intended* to make a confession. But also it is not permissable to look at other facts which might not be known at the time or which might emerge in evidence at the trial. The conditions under which a confession can be admitted as evidence vary in different countries. In the old ecclesiastical courts under the Continental system of inquisitorial law, confession was accepted as a sure proof of guilt and many thousands of witches, for example, were put to death after confessing under torture. Even in Great Britain confessions were got by duress, although torture was forbidden under English common law. It is now recognized in civilized countries that a 'confession' made under torture is valueless as evidence of guilt.

A confession is admissable under English law as evidence against an accused person provided it has not been obtained under duress, or extorted – by threats or promises of favour. To be admissable a confession must be free and voluntary. 'If it proceeds from remorse and a desire to make reparation for the crime, it is admissible. If it flows from hope or fear, incited by a person in authority, it is inadmissable' (Reg. v Thompson, 1893). For this reason the police are required to caution a person before making a charge by saying, 'Do you wish to say anything in answer to the charge? You are not obliged to say anything unless you wish to do so, but whatever you say will be taken down in writing, and may be used as evidence against you.' In some countries (Ceylon) no confession made to a police officer is admissible as evidence against a person accused of any offence.

Comparative Religion
5. Confession (sacramental or auricular confession) is the declaration by a penitent of his sins in the presence of a priest. Confession is found in many oriental and primitive religions, including that of ancient Babylon. When all troubles and afflictions were regarded as punishments by the gods for transgressions, confession in a Temple was

a means of seeking relief. In the Anglican and other Churches, confession is voluntary, but permitted in private in the presence of a priest. As practised in the Roman Catholic Church, confession is compulsory and the priest is held to be divinely invested with authority to forgive sins by granting 'absolution.'

CONGENITAL

Medicine
This word is a source of misunderstanding, since it is used sometimes to imply a causal mechanism and sometimes to indicate a time relationship.
1. Present in an individual from time of birth; connate. The word is used in this sense for example in *congenital syphilis*, due to infection before birth and in *congenital paraplegia*, which may result from a birth injury.
2. Hereditary; attributable to the hereditary constitution. Many congenital disorders are of this kind.

CONSCIENCE. CONSCIENTIOUS

Common Language
Conscience is an inner feeling of right and wrong in an individual's personal actions and motives, coupled with the desire to do what is right. A guilty conscience is an unpleasant feeling that may be experienced. It may be experienced after an action or thought believed to be sinful or wrong. In some persons conscience appears to play a very little part, while in others it is an important factor in their lives. It can be strong enough to lead a murderer to confess and accept the consequences of his crime.

In the past the 'voice of conscience' was commonly attributed to mysterious supernatural agencies such as 'the voice of God', but it is now generally accepted that conscience can be explained in psychological terms. One of the factors contributing to conscience is believed to be (a) fear of discovery. Thus there is evidence that a guilty conscience is generally less troublesome if there is absolutely no fear of being found out. Another factor is (b) fear of losing self-esteem, for no-one likes to fall too far short of his idea of perfection. A third factor is (c) uneasiness over deviating from the habitual behaviour pattern of right doing built up in the early formative years of life. Sigmund Freud showed how environmental experiences in early life build up a system of values existing as a directive mechanism (the 'super-ego') in the unconscious mind and he concluded that conscience 'in its origin is dread of the community and nothing else'. In support of this view one of the main facts about the 'voice of conscience' is that it is not consistent. 'We know that conscience enjoins different acts in different parts of the world, and that broadly speaking it is everywhere in agreement with tribal custom.' (Bertrand Russell, *The Conquest of Happiness*). Thus one man's conscience may tell him to act in one way, while another man's conscience will direct him otherwise: but the conscience generally correlates closely with the social system and upbringing in an individual's early environment. In most people the conscience can also be modified by suggestion. Thus killing, which normally would cause a guilty conscience, is readily accepted as right in time of war. The belief that a guilty conscience can be eased by confession and penance is accepted by many adherents of certain religions, and acting in that belief they are able to silence a guilty conscience and so behave as if lacking in conscience. A guilty conscience can also be relieved for example by sending a donation *(conscience money)* after evasions of income tax.

The word *conscientious* which literally means being obedient to the dictates of conscience, is now commonly used in a broader sense for an attitude or behaviour which is careful, painstaking and considerate. In the term *conscientious objector*, which denotes those who refuse to perform compulsory military service, the conscience is taken to be the reason for their behaviour, which is generally based on the firm belief that violence and warfare are wrong. In this belief they may be influenced by ethical and intellectual as well as by religious considerations. The strength of conscience over this issue is indicated by the records of many early Christians who refused to join the Roman armies and

76

sooner accepted the penalty of death. There were in fact many in those days who, because of their conscientious objections, were executed or thrown to the lions.

CONTRACT

Common Language
1. A contract is a mutual promise or voluntary agreement that can be enforced by the law. Thus one person may agree with another to deliver goods or perform some service in return for a specified payment; if a contract is created, the agreement then becomes legally binding on both of them. A contract makes obligations for all the parties to it; and each party has the legal right to insist that the other parties fulfil the obligations stated in the contract. It should be noted that obligations of a social, moral or honorary kind do not create a contract in law. In the Common Language the word 'contract' is used both for the agreement and the document in which the agreement is defined.

Law
2. 'A contract is an agreement enforceable by law, made between two or more persons, by which rights are acquired by one or more to acts or forbearances on the part of the other or others' (Sir William Anson).

In English law, for a contract to be created an offer and an acceptance of the offer must both be communicated between the parties. The offer can be withdrawn by giving notice of retraction at any time before the offer is accepted. The acceptance must be absolute, in the same terms as the offer, and not partial or conditional. Silence does not mean acceptance. A letter of acceptance is effective as soon as it is posted, provided that the accepting party has not previously received a notice of retraction.

The parties to a contract must be reasonably supposed to believe that the offer and acceptance are legally binding. An *express contract* is a contract made in writing (in a deed signed, sealed and delivered). An *implied contract* is a contract created by oral exchange of words and inferred from the conduct of the parties, when supported by a consideration that the agreement confers a benefit on one party or a forbearance on the part of the other, and is not merely for gratuitous services. A *voidable contract* is one that may be rendered void or held valid at the option of one of the parties.

For a contract to be binding, the parties to it must have the capacity to enter into it. Thus a city corporation must contract under its seal. Persons under the age of eighteen (infants) cannot generally be held liable on account of contracts made by them, but contracts for necessaries and for an infant's benefit are legally binding. A contract may be held to be unenforceable, if made (a) under a mistake, (b) as a result of undue influence or coercion, or (c) as a result of misrepresentation. But impossibility of performance is not accepted as a substantial ground for avoiding a contract. If a person agrees unconditionally to do something that ultimately turns out to be impossible, he can still be held to his contract and he may also have to pay damages for failure to fulfil the obligations he has undertaken to perform.

An agreement to do anything illegal (sometimes called a 'void' contract) is not a contract in law, and the parties do not gain contractual rights or liabilities. Thus an agreement to commit a crime, to trade with the enemy, or to commit an immoral offence is not a valid contract.

There is an important difference between a contract *for* service and a contract *of* service. In a contract *for* service the master can order or require what is to be done: in a contract *of* service, he can not only order or require what is to be done, but he can also direct how it shall be done.

The laws of contract differ to some extent in different countries and there are significant differences between the English and Scots law. In English law, contracts relating to land in another country must conform to the regulations in force in the country where the land is situated.

Marriage is a special form of contract, since it involves a change of status on the part of the parties concerned. The laws regulating the contractual capacity for marriage vary widely in different countries: a marriage that would be valid in one country may therefore be invalid in another.

CONTROL

Common Language
This word is used in a number of different senses:
1. The fact of checking, controlling, regulating, coordinating or restraining any activity.
2. A method, system, mechanism or instrument for checking or regulating any process or activity.
3. Direction, domination, command.

Economics
4. The regulation by the State of commercial or financial dealings, supplies of raw materials, etc. for the purpose of upholding the interests of the community and preventing abuses, such as the exploitation of the community by private interests. Such controls limit the range of free action of private individuals where that is regarded as being in the public interest.

Experimental science
5. A control is a procedure introduced into an experiment for the purpose of limiting the number of variables under observation, and so increasing the validity of any inference that may be drawn. Thus in an experiment designed to observe the effects of any specific treatment on a group of experimental subjects, it may be advantageous to make similar observations on a second group of untreated subjects (known as control subjects). In this way it is made more probable that any observed effects are attributable to the treatment given, and not to extraneous or chance factors beyond the experimenter's control. The likelihood of a *post hoc fallacy* is thereby reduced.

The planning of suitable controls is an important part of the design of many biological experiments. In some experiments it may be appropriate to make observations on a random sample taken from the same population as the experimental sample. In other experiments it may be preferable to select control subjects matched for age, sex, weight or other variable factors. By the use of littermates in animal experiments the variation in genetic endowment may be controlled. A control is sometimes carried out by making observations on the same subjects as are used for the experimental group, but at a time when they are not being submitted to the experimental treatment.

A series of observations or measurements made for the purpose of testing equipment, calibrating apparatus or checking the conditions of the main experiment, or otherwise validating experimental results, may be regarded as a separate control experiment.

Psychic research
6. The term 'control' is given to a spirit believed to be manifested through a medium.

CRUELTY

Common Language
1. Cruelty is behaviour that inflicts pain on another without proper reason. The word is also used loosely in a number of different senses to describe (2) any act which causes suffering, (3) the character of a cruel act, (4) the disposition of a person who inflicts pain and (5) cruelty as a form of vice or perversion.

The word 'cruelty' is also used in another sense to describe (6) indifference to, or pleasure in, another's pain (German: *Schadenfreude*). Cruelty may be physical or mental and it can apply to animals as well as to persons and communities. We can speak of the cruelty of a law or of an Act of Parliament; we can also speak of the cruelty of the human race or the cruelty of a disease. The concept of cruelty is complicated in that it involves the judgement of a third person.

Law
7. The definition of cruelty is important in relation to actions for divorce in countries which accept cruelty as grounds for divorce. In Gollins v Gollins (1962) Lord Justice Willmer said:

'The propositions of law which must be considered in dealing with allegations of cruelty are few and relatively simple.

80

'First. The conduct complained of must be such as to cause danger to health, bodily or mental, or a reasonable apprehension thereof.

'Second. Conduct on the part of the offending spouse must be in some sense aimed at or directed against the complaining spouse. Where the Court found the conduct was pursued with actual intention to injure, no further inquiry was necessary; but such an intention could be inferred where, e.g. the conduct was persisted in (a) after a warning that it was having an adverse effect on the other spouse, or (b) in circumstances in which a reasonable person would appreciate that it was likely to injure the other spouse. Any spouse may be presumed to intend the nature and consequences of his own behaviour. Thus any course of conduct intentionally pursued, provided it had some impact on the other spouse, may in appropriate circumstances justify a finding of cruelty.

'Third. If the above two requirements were not satisfied, the charge of cruelty was not made out and must as a matter of law be dismissed.

'Fourth. If they were satisfied, then the question of whether the conduct did amount to cruelty was one of fact and degree to be decided in the light of the circumstances of the particular case. Regard must be had to the considerations that a charge of cruelty was a serious one and that it was always necessary to consider the personality of the two spouses, and in particular the physical and mental condition and susceptibilities of the innocent spouse.'

He concluded that neglect in failing to maintain a spouse or their children could constitute cruelty in law.

8. The Cruelty to Animals Act (1876) in England relates to experiments on living vertebrate animals (other than man) calculated to cause pain. A procedure is defined as calculated to cause pain if it is liable to interfere in a material degree with the animal's health, comfort or integrity.

DEATH

Common Language
The word is used for (1) the fact or process of dying, as in a quick or a slow death. (2) The cessation of life in a part, or the complete cessation of life of a living organism, as shown by the loss of vital functions such as consciousness, breathing, pulse and response to painful stimuli.

Medicine
For scientific purposes the primitive view that an organism can exist in only two possible conditions, alive or dead, is clearly inadequate. Nor is it correct to regard life as being extinguished abruptly at 'the moment of death'. In actual fact dying is a gradual process that occurs unevenly in different parts of the body and it takes place over an appreciable period of time. One organ may die before another and some of the vital functions of the body may persist when many of the cells are already dead. It is possible therefore to distinguish for example between (3) 'heart death', when the heart has ceased to function, and (4) 'brain death', when irreversible brain damage has occurred. The distinction is of practical importance in view of the possibility of maintaining life in some cases by the use of artificial respiration and circulation machines.

It is now generally agreed that for the overt expression of a living personality brain function is essential and that therefore brain death constitutes the most valid index of death in man. In 1968 a committee set up by the Harvard Medical School to examine the definition of death stressed the following criteria: (1) the total lack of awareness of and response to external stimuli; (2) the absence of breathing as judged by one hour of observation or by the absence of spontaneous breathing efforts when the mechanical respiration is turned off for three minutes; (3) the absence of reflex responses; (4) absence of spontaneous electrical activity of the brain ('flat EEG') and (5) the absence of circulation as judged by the standstill of blood in the retinal vessels of the eye or absence of heart activity (*Journal of the American Medical Association*, vol. *205*, p.337, 1968). They considered that the tests should be repeated twenty-four hours or more later, but regarded the criteria of death as valid only in the absence of hypothermia or of barbiturates or other central depressant drugs.

More recent investigations have drawn attention to cases of cardiac arrest in which the parts of the brain required for spontaneous respiration and for certain brain-stem reflexes have survived, although the cerebral cortex has been irreparably destroyed as shown by the persistent absence of electrical activity and absence of sensory evoked cortical responses (Brierley *et al* 1971). Such cases of (6) 'neocortical death' do not conform to the criteria of death proposed by the Harvard committee, but once neocortical death has been unequivocally established and the possibility of any recovery of consciousness and intellectual activity thereby excluded, the condition can hardly be regarded as other than one that should be included in the different forms of death.

Morbidity statistics
The causes of death are not always easily defined. Thus an abnormality, injury, poisoning or disease may lead ultimately to death by heart failure, by bleeding or by exhaustion. Often there are two or more contributory causes which can be described in different ways. The World Health Organization has recommended a standard international terminology for defining the causes of death in morbidity statistics (*Manual of the International Statistical Classification of Diseases, Injuries and Causes of Death*, 1957, vol. 1, WHO, Geneva).

DEFAMATION

Common Language
1. Defamation is the act of making a public assertion, whether true or false, which injures the reputation of another person.

Law
2. In British law, a statement is defamatory if (a) directly or (b) by innuendo, the words tend to bring a person into

dislike, contempt or ridicule in the eyes of right-thinking men generally. It was ruled by Mr Justice McNair (1963) that the words complained of must be construed in their natural and ordinary meaning as ordinary and intelligent men would understand them, and they must be words which disparage a person's reputation in the eyes of right-thinking men generally. To write or say of a man something that will disparage him in the eyes of a particular group or section of the community, but which will not affect his reputation in the eyes of the average right-thinking man, is not actionable within the law of defamation.

DELUSION

Common Language
1. A delusion is a false belief which cannot be corrected by an appeal to reason, and which is not attributable to exceptional upbringing, circumstances or surroundings.

Psychiatry
2. Delusions can arise by false reasoning, or by reasoning correctly from hallucinations or illusions.

Primary delusions (Gruhle, 1915) appear, fully developed, as a sudden conviction. Thus some trivial observation or event, such as a BBC announcement, may be felt to be of vital significance in indicating the imminent end of the world. The experience comes without warning and it may puzzle the patient. Primary delusions indicate a disturbance of symbolization which may be of a neurological type or at a fundamental level.

Interpretative delusions are secondary symptoms. They represent an attempt to adapt to the conditions imposed by a deeper primary disorder. They arise from the inner emotional needs: they are therefore not amenable to logic. Generally they develop gradually and progress with the development of the primary disorder. Delusions may relate to the environment, to the bodily functions or to the personality of the patient: they may appear rational, or they may be wildly irrational and bizarre in type. Common varieties are hypochondriacal delusions, and delusions of grandeur and of persecution, which often go together. Delusions which fit in with each other so as to make a coherent story, logical within itself, are described as *systematized delusions*.

DEMOCRACY. DEMOCRATIC

Common Language
Coming from the Greek *demos*, the people, and *kratos*, rule, democracy means (1) rule by the people. Abraham Lincoln defined democracy as 'government of the people by the people for the people': but different interpretations can be given to an expression which does not state who exactly are 'the people' or how they are to govern. The term 'democracy' has been applied to many different systems which give the common people a voice in the government, and the concept of democracy has varied widely in different countries at different times. In the Common Language the terms 'democracy' and 'democratic' are applied loosely to (2) a *form of government* carried out by elected representatives of the people, (3) the *principles* underlying a democratic form of government and (4) a *community* or *state* governed by democratic rule. In contexts other than national government democracy is (5) a type of *social relationship* in which all are accepted as equal and accorded equal rights, irrespective of wealth, rank, colour, caste, sex or creed. Democracy can also mean (6) upholding the interests and wishes of the majority of the people rather than those of a privileged few in the management of an organisation such as a business, a union or a club. Democracy has been called 'the voice of the people' and it can mean simply (7) the assertion of ordinary people's views and rights.

Politics
Democracy was at one time (8) a form of government in which the power was held collectively by the people and exercised by them directly, and not by their representatives. This form of government which is sometimes described as *direct democracy* was practised in the fifth century BC in Athens, where the citizens met

periodically for the making of laws. Direct democracy still operates at the present day in the use of the *referendum* in Switzerland, Belgium and in certain states of the USA.

Democracy is (9) a form of government in which the ultimate power is held collectively by the whole people, but exercised by officers freely elected by them as their representatives. The idea that the power should be in the hands of the *whole* people is the view of democracy which is now currently held in most European countries and in the United States: but this represents a relatively recent concept, for in most countries until the nineteenth century the working classes were largely excluded from the electorate. In the democracy of ancient Athens 'the people' were restricted to the relatively small number of Greeks and did not include their numerous slaves. Women were included in England only in 1918, but they had to be thirty or more years of age: they are still excluded from the electorate in Switzerland.

The kind of democracy in which the power is exercised by representatives of the people, sometimes described as *indirect democracy*, depends very much on the way in which the representatives are elected. The freedom to nominate representatives, free elections by secret ballot, free speech and free press are inherent in the concept of *western democracy* currently held in England, France and the USA. However, in some countries criticism of the existing government is made a criminal offence and dissidents opposed to the existing government are not permitted to stand for election. Although such countries may claim to be upholding the interests of the common people and describe themselves as democratic, under those conditions democracy has a differnt meaning. In the United Kingdom free speech is permitted and government by the people's elected representatives is limited only by a veto in the House of Lords.

Democracy is sometimes taken to imply that the views and wishes of the majority must invariably prevail: but this cannot always be done, since the wishes of the majority sometimes change and they are often inconsistent. There are also technical matters which the people are not qualified to judge. In such matters it is not inconsistent with democracy that experts should be empowered to decide. This is in fact what happens in the United Kingdom in Parliament, which is often ahead of the majority in its views, and which exercises the principles of *Parliamentary democracy*. In the United States the President is democratically elected, but the powers of the executive government are restricted by the written Constitution and by the doctrine of State Rights. In the United States the terms 'democracy' and 'democratic' are often used in a narrower sense for (10) the principles of the Democratic Party, which aims at upholding the interests of the common man as opposed to the interests of 'big business' supported by the Republican Party.

In the USSR, Communist Asia and other Democratic Soviet States democracy is (11) a form of government in which the ultimate power is held by a political party under a single party system and exercised for the benefit of the people by officers who are not freely elected by the people: the power of the Party is maintained by political control, including censorship of the press. This 'Eastern' concept of democracy is of relatively recent origin: it differs widely from the older concepts of democracy and those which are current of the countries of the Western World. It is significant that the term 'undemocratic' is commonly used by the Soviet authorities to mean 'against the State'.

DEPRESSION

Common Language
1. The word depression is used in different senses to describe a relative lowering in level, in quality, in quantity, in activity, etc. For example, a depression in a plane (concavity); a trade depression; depression of spirits (dejection).

Astronomy
2. The angle of depression is the angle made with the horizontal plane by a straight line extending from the observer to a point below the horizon. Conversely, the angle

made by a point above the horizontal plane is the angle of elevation or altitude.

Meteorology
3. A depression is a temporary lowering in atmospheric pressure. The magnitude of the depression may be expressed by the decrease in height of a column of mercury in a barometer.
4. A depression is a mobile system of winds rotating around a centre of low barometric pressure: a cyclone.

Psychology
5. Depression is a mood characterized by feelings of sadness, discouragement, inadequacy and self-reproach, associated with lack of zest, lack of initiative, reduced activity, gloomy thoughts and pessimistic outlook. It is described also as dejection. Depression may occur as a normal reaction to serious loss or to frustration of a major drive.

Psychiatry
The word 'depression' is used in psychiatry to describe various forms of illness in which a depressive mood is the dominant symptom.

A diagnosis of depressive illness is commonly made on the basis of a syndrome which includes a varying proportion of the following symptoms: (a) a depression of mood, (b) disturbance of sleep, (c) loss of appetite, (d) lack of energy, (e) thoughts of suicide (f) feelings of unworthiness and of guilt, (g) retardation of response, (h) restlessness and agitation, (i) weeping, (j) tension or anxiety, (k) gastro-intestinal symptoms, (l) loss of libido, (m) hypochondriacal fears (n) loss of weight, (o) loss of insight, (p) reduced working efficiency, (q) inability to experience enjoyment, (r) inability to change mood in response to environmental stimuli, (s) delusions, (t) hallucinations.

Depressive illnesses were formerly considered to fall into two main classes - *Neurotic Depression* and *Psychotic Depression*: but it is now believed that these differ mainly in the severity of the symptoms and that no clear distinction can be drawn between them. Another old classification, also based on

88

clinical symptoms, distinguishes between *Agitated Depression*, in which the patient is characteristically restless or irritable, and *Retarded Depression*, characterized by slowness and hesitation in responding to stimuli.

There have been many attempts to classify depressive disorders on an aetiological basis according to the causal factors which give rise to them, but there is no general agreement as to how depressive illnesses are caused or how they should be classified. In some cases external environmental factors are apparently important, whereas in other cases endogenous factors appear to play a major role. It is generally recognized that depressive illness is influenced by a number of different causal factors which probably operate to some extent in every case: they include the basic personality, inborn hereditary factors, the course of maturation and development, general physical health and provoking environmental factors. The following forms of depressive illness have been described.

6. *Reactive Depressions (Depressive Reactions, Neurotic Depressions)* are depressive states following directly on a painful experience: the thought content is centred on the provoking emotional experience, and the symptoms are pathological in that they exceed in intensity or duration the reaction which might normally be expected.

7. *Endogenous Depressions* are depressive states attributable mainly to endogenous constitutional factors and in which external provocative causes play only a minimal part. The depression which occurs spontaneously in the depressive phases of a manic-depressive psychosis is commonly regarded as endogenous in origin, although the causal mechanisms may be different from those in other forms of endogenous depression.

8. *Organic depressions* are depressive states associated with demonstrable organic lesions of the brain: they occur in cases of brain injury, cerebral tumours, presenile dementia, general paresis and cerebrovascular disease.

9. *Symptomatic depressions* are depressive states occurring as symptoms of general physical illnesses and in toxic states: they may occur, for example, after infective diseases such as influenza, in association with endocrine disturbances (premenstrual, puerperal, menopausal, etc.), after taking

certain drugs (sulphonamides, reserepine, etc.) and after withdrawal of drugs of addiction. The name *Involutional Depression* is given to depressive states which commonly occur in men and women at the time of the climacteric. Some authorities have used the term *Exhaustive Depression* for depressive states resulting from long-continued agitation or emotional strain.

DIAGNOSIS

Medicine
1. Diagnosis is the art or practice of determining the nature of a disease condition by recognizing the characteristic signs and symptoms that may be present. The discrimination between a number of different diseases by comparing and contrasting their symptoms is known as *differential diagnosis*. The methods used in diagnosis include (a) the study of the nature and history of the signs and symptoms, (b) the clinical examination of the patient and (c) investigation by special methods such as biochemical or physical tests or X-ray photography.
2. The word 'diagnosis' is also used for a statement of opinion about a disease condition in any particular patient. If the nature of the disease is evident on first inspection a *'spot diagnosis'* may be made at once. If there is insufficient information for a confident diagnosis to be made at the time when the patient is first seen, the physician may make a *provisional diagnosis*, which can serve as a basis for treatment until a definite diagnosis can be made later. An opinion based on the results of laboratory investigations of blood, urine, etc. is known as *laboratory diagnosis*. Terms such as *X-ray diagnosis*, and *biological diagnosis* are applied to opinions based on special methods of investigation.

Different types of diagnosis differ greatly in the amount of information they convey. Thus the following different types of diagnosis may be distinguished:

(a) Descriptive diagnoses (e.g. 'jaundice', 'depression') express simply the signs or symptoms that are present. A diagnosis of this type is equivalent to a 'label' in giving a name to the condition without giving any further information about it. A set of associated symptoms is known as a *syndrome*.

(b) Diagnoses expressing the organ mainly affected (e.g. 'appendicitis', 'gastritis', 'arthritis').

(c) Diagnoses giving the general nature of the condition (e.g. 'venereal disease', 'avitaminosis').

(d) Diagnoses giving the causative agency (e.g. 'anthrax', 'tuberculosis').

(e) Composite diagnoses giving information of more than one kind. These include many of the technical forms of diagnosis commonly used by the medical profession. They are of particular value since they enable a disease condition to be defined with greater precision (e.g. 'pneumococcal meningitis', 'macrocytic anaemia', 'dissecting aneurysm of the abdominal aorta').

DISEASE

Common Language
1. The word is used in a general sense as a collective term for any departure from a state of health in living organisms. Thus we may speak of the ravages of disease. In this sense disease includes conditions such as infestation by parasites and blight in plants.
2. The word is used also in a narrower sense for any particular form of physical illness or morbid condition, generally with a characteristic train of symptoms, such as tuberculosis or cancer in animals and man, or virus disease in plants. The words *malady* and *ailment*, which are similar in meaning, are no longer in very common use.

Medicine
3. The current concepts of disease have developed mainly through the observation that there is a relation between the signs and symptoms of illness seen at the bedside and the pathological changes in the body found after death. A disease may therefore be defined as a condition in which normal functions of the body are progressively impaired by a pathological process. A disease generally gives rise to a succession of characteristic signs and symptoms; but it may

91

be symptomless during life and detected only after death. Conditions regarded as diseases are generally restricted to those in which the symptoms are attributable to a definite pathological process such as a bacterial or viral infection, a growth or a specific metabolic dysfunction that can be defined. A disease process may be active or quiescent at different times. We can thus speak of the natural history of a disease, describing its mode of onset, course and ultimate outcome. The condition during a period of quiescence, when symptoms are mainly absent, is sometimes described as *latent disease*.

Conditions in which (a) a group of symptoms recur from time to time without a marked progression and (b) where symptoms occur without any known cause, are commonly described as *disorders* rather than as diseases: such conditions include migraine, asthma, headache, epilepsy and various forms of mental illness. *Pathological conditions* (c) due to physical injury or poisoning, and (d) *disabilities* present from the time of birth, are also generally classed as disorders: such conditions include for example, burns, delirium tremens, carbon monoxide poisoning, congenital deformities and mental subnormality.

It is usual to distinguish between a definite disease entity and (e) a *symptom-complex*, which is a group of symptoms occurring together, and (f) a *syndrome*, which is a set of signs and symptoms occurring in characteristic sequence, but in which the nature of the underlying disease process is not definitely established.

Diseases may be classified in many different ways, depending on the way in which the subject is approached. Thus the medical practitioner may classify them primarily according to their treatment into medical and surgical divisions: the anatomist according to the part of the body affected; the pathologist according to the nature of the underlying pathological process; and the statistician so that reliable quantitative data may be obtained about groups of cases suffering from similar conditions. For purposes of statistical classification, the recognized categories of disease must be restricted to a limited number of groups which will cover the whole range of morbid conditions. A medical nomenclature, on the other hand, differs from this in that it is essentially a list of agreed terms for describing clinical and pathological conditions observed in individual cases; and it needs to be so extensive that any specific pathological condition can be accurately recorded.

A standard international classification of disease, injuries and causes of death (1957) adopted for statistical purposes by the World Health Assembly in 1955 is published by the World Health Organization, Geneva. It contains seventeen main divisions which are subdivided into smaller sub-categories. The diseases and disorders forming the main divisions are:

I. Infective and parasitic diseases.
II. Neoplasms (growths).
III. Allergic, endocrine, metabolic and nutritional diseases.
IV. Diseases of the blood and blood-forming organs.
V. Mental, psychoneurotic and personality disorders.
VI. Diseases of the nervous system and sense organs.
VII. Circulatory diseases.
VIII. Respiratory diseases.
IX. Diseases of the digestive system.
X. Genito-urinary diseases.
XI. Deliveries and complications of pregnancy, child-birth and the puerperium.
XII. Diseases of skin and cellular tissue.
XIII. Diseases of the bones and organs of movement.
XIV. Congenital malformations.
XV. Diseases of early infancy.
XVI. Symptoms, senility and ill-defined conditions.
XVII. Accidents, poisoning and violence.

DOGMA. DOGMATIC

1. A dogma is a teaching or belief which, although unproven, is firmly held and asserted on inadequate evidence to be true. A strongly held teaching or belief based on doubtful evidence may be described as dogmatic. The word 'dogmatic' is also used to describe the assertive, authoritative or arrogant attitudes of persons who tena-

ciously uphold and insist on the truth of teachings and beliefs for which the evidence is unsatisfactory.

2. The religious doctrines of the churches based on divine revelation and regarded by some as incontrovertibly true, have been classed by others as dogmas and contrasted with scientific truths, which are based on direct observation and reason, but which by definition must still be approached with an open mind.

DRUG

Common Language
The word is commonly used in two different senses.

1. A drug is a 'medicine': a substance used medicinally by itself or as an ingredient in a pharmaceutical preparation to cure, alleviate, diagnose or prevent disease.

2. A drug is a substance that can affect the way a person feels. In the lay mind drugs are often associated with depravity and addiction. A drug is then conceived as a substance with a powerful and possibly sinister action on the brain. The highly addictive or 'hard' drugs include opiates and narcotics; for example morphine, heroin and cocaine. Less addictive or 'soft' drugs include hashish, barbiturates and derivatives of amphetamine. A third class of drugs includes substances taken because they may produce hallucinations or may in other ways alter a person's relation to reality; for example mescaline and LSD. Drugs of this kind have been used in religious ceremonies in the belief that they can induce mystical experiences.

Law
For legal purposes it may be necessary to define different classes of drugs and to determine, for example, whether a pharmaceutical preparation should be classed as a drug or as a food, a toilet preparation or a disinfectant. Thus in the UK it is recommended in the National Health Service Regulations of October 1951 that disinfectants should be regarded as drugs only when they are prescribed in such quantities and with such directions as are appropriate for

the treatment of an individual patient, either internally or externally; and that disinfectants should not be regarded as drugs if they are ordered for general hygienic purposes. Some different classes of drugs are detailed in the definition of 'drug' given in the New Zealand Food and Drug Act of 1969:

3. A drug is '(a) Any substance or mixture of substances used or represented for use, whether internally or externally, for the purpose of the prevention, diagnosis, or treatment of any disease, ailment, disorder, deformity, defect, or injury of the human body;

   (b) Any substance or mixture of substances used or represented for use for the purpose of altering the shape or structure of the human body;

   (c) Any substance or mixture of substances, including anaesthetics, used or represented for use for the purposes of influencing, inhibiting or modifying any physiological process in human beings or the desires or emotions connected with any such physiological process, or the desire for alcohol or tobacco;

   (d) Any chemical contraceptive;

   (e) Any material used or represented for use as surgical dressing;

   (f) Any disinfectant, germicide, or antiseptic;

   (g) Any tobacco prepared for smoking, chewing or snuffing.'

Pharmacology
The World Health Organization Expert Committee on Drug Dependence (1969) defined a drug as (4) 'any substance that, when taken into the living organism, may modify one or more of its functions'.

ENERGY

Common Language
1. Physical or mental vigour. The capacity for strenuous exertion.

Physics
2. Energy may be defined as the capacity for doing work.

The word was first introduced into physics in 1807 by Thomas Young, who used it in a restricted sense to denote the energy associated with motion, or the *kinetic energy* of a moving body. ('The term energy may be applied . . . to the product of the mass or weight of a body, into the square of the number expressing its velocity.')

Since the recognition that heat and kinetic energy are interconvertible, the meaning of the word has been extended to include heat, light and other forms of energy. Thus, heat is converted in a steam engine into kinetic energy, which can be made to do work. Conversely, when a moving body is stopped by friction, the kinetic energy is converted into heat. Since heat, or thermal energy, is due to the movement of molecules, it may be regarded as another form of kinetic energy. Energy can neither be created nor destroyed: the only changes of which we have knowledge are changes of one form of energy into another.

Potential energy is the energy possessed by a body by reason of its position in a gravitational field, or in any other field of force. Chemical energy may be regarded as potential energy at a molecular level. When a bullet is fired from a gun, the chemical energy of the gunpowder is converted partly into thermal energy and partly into the kinetic energy of the bullet. In an electric battery, chemical energy is converted into electrical energy. Nuclear energy is the energy derived from transformations within the nucleus of an atom.

EPILEPSY

Common Language
1. Epilepsy is commonly conceived as an incurable hereditary disease in which the sufferer is liable at any time to fall to the ground in a violent fit: this idea of epilepsy differs from the modern medical view, but it is still widely held. Epilepsy used to be called 'the falling sickness': in ancient times it was believed to be due to possession by devils, and it was regarded with superstitious fear and shame, but that view is no longer held.

Medicine
2. Epilepsy is the name given to a group of chronic disorders of the brain characterized by sudden short attacks (fits, seizures, ictuses) occurring at intervals. The fits take many different forms, depending on the parts of the brain that are affected and the way in which the functions of the brain are disturbed: involuntary movements and loss of consciousness generally occur both together or alone. An epileptic fit sometimes starts with a sensory disturbance, such as an abnormal taste, smell or visual impression, which is known as an *aura*. A fit may last from a few seconds to several minutes, and it is often followed by a period of (*post-ictal*) confusion, or depression. The frequency of the fits varies greatly in different cases and in the same cases at different times, ranging from less than one a year to one every few minutes: but in many cases the fits can now be greatly reduced in number, or entirely prevented by modern methods of medical and surgical treatment, so that the consequences of epilepsy are no longer as serious as they used to be.

The epilepsies may be classified in various different ways: if classified according to the pattern of the seizure and other symptoms, the following types may be recognized:

(a) *Major* (or *grand mal*) *epilepsy*. This is the most severe form of epilepsy, in which the seizures generally take the form of violent tonic and clonic convulsions with complete loss of consciousness. The patient may cry out at the start and may injure himself in falling or cause injury to others: he is mentally confused for a time after regaining consciousness. When grand mal seizures occur repeatedly in quick succession, so that the patient barely has time to regain consciousness in between them, the condition is known as *status epilepticus*. This is a serious condition which may be fatal if it is not quickly treated.

(b) *Minor* (or *petit mal*) epilepsy. The seizures take the form of momentary loss of consciousness (blackouts or absences) lasting for not more than a few seconds. There are no convulsions and generally no involuntary movements of the limbs: the patient does not generally fall, but there may be a

97

change in muscular tone, as shown for example, by a momentary sagging at the knees. Minor seizures with no involuntary movements are said to be *akinetic* in type; or if they are very frequent, *pyknoleptic*: when accompanied by twitching of the smaller muscles of the face or hands, they are described as minor seizures of *myoclonic* type.

(c) *Local (Jacksonian) epilepsy.* In this form of epilepsy described by Hughlings Jackson, involuntary convulsive movements occur, starting typically on one side of the body only, without impairment of consciousness.

(d) *Psychomotor epilepsy.* The actual fit is not generally severe in type and it may escape notice: but in the subsequent post-ictal period the patient is liable to behave irrationally and he may carry out acts which he cannot afterwards remember (automatism).

(e) *Sensory epilepsy.* Sensory fits may take the form of visual, auditory or other types of hallucinations and they may be referred to any part of the body. Thus a sensation of 'numbness' or 'tingling' may spread through the limbs: epigastric sensations and vertigo are relatively common. Such disturbances may occur as the sole indication of epilepsy. The disturbance may also spread into wider areas of the brain, involving generalized convulsions: the sensory disturbance is then described as a warning or *aura* of the major fit.

(f) Mixed forms of epilepsy are relatively common. Thus a patient may have frequent minor fits and occasional major seizures. Seizures intermediate between minor and major fits are also found: loss of consciousness may be regularly associated with falling or with muscular spasm, but with generalized convulsions. Twitchings of muscles in different parts of the body, known as *jacitation*, occur from time to time in many epileptics.

ESTABLISHMENT

Common Language
1. Establishment (from the Latin *Stabilis*, standing firm) is the act or process of setting up an organisation, institution, office, post, service, premises, etc. for the carrying out of

some specific activity. Establishment may consist of obtaining official recognition from a competent authority or ensuring the continuation of financial support.

2. In another sense of the word, an establishment is something established, such as a business, a Government department, a household, a staff, a church, or any organisation recognized officially by a state.

3. The Establishment (generally spelt with an initial capital letter) is the aggregate of organisations constituting the main social fabric and power structure of a country. It generally includes the armed forces, financial and industrial concerns, churches and professional bodies. The relative importance of these different sections of the community varies in different countries. In some countries the churches have great power and play a leading role in the Establishment; in others the armed forces or the financial interests are dominant. The views of the Establishment often differ from those of minority groups in a country.

Psychology
Permanent components of the personality structure such as Freud's *ego, id,* and *super ego* have been described as establishments by some psychologists.

EVIDENCE

Common Language
1. Statements, documents or information of any kind that can serve as a basis for belief, or that can influence opinion in judging an issue. The derivation of the word from the Latin *videre* 'to see' is a reminder that evidence generally implies something that has been seen or heard, and not gossip, rumour, opinions, unauthenticated writings, or authoritarian views.

It should be noted that the word is used with different meanings in scientific, legal and religious contexts. In legal writings emphasis is generally placed on the concept of 'proof', and the evidence is sometimes taken to include the proof as well as the information cited in support of it. In scientific work evidence is used rather to estimate a probability. In religious writings (apologetics), the criteria of reliability of evidence differ from those in science and in the courts of justice.

Law
2. Testimony by word of mouth, documents, etc. cited to prove an allegation or point at issue between two parties. Several different classes of evidence are recognized, and the significance of the different kinds of evidence depends on the rules of procedure, which vary to some extent in different countries. In English law, the chief general rules of procedure are: (a) Only evidence that is relevant to the point at issue may be produced: no irrelevant evidence is admitted. (b) An assertion must be proved by the party who makes it. (c) The evidence produced on any point must be the best obtainable. Thus the contents of a deed must be proved by producing the original deed, and not a copy of the deed or a verbal statement of the contents. The best obtainable evidence is sometimes described as *primary* evidence, and the more remote evidence as *secondary*. (d) *Hearsay* evidence is not admitted, except in special circumstances. The evidence is sometimes taken to include the facts cited and also the proof.
3. *Oral evidence (parole or word-of-mouth testimony)*. A statement of fact may be made by a witness under oath about what he has seen, heard or otherwise knows: a witness's opinion is not evidence. The evidence of a witness can be admitted in a court of justice only (a) if the witness is capable of understanding the subject of his testimony and (b) if he is judged to have sufficient moral principle to speak the truth. Testimony must be given under oath unless the witness claims the right to testify as an atheist. In English law, a witness cannot generally be asked any questions as to previous charges, convictions or bad character, and he is not compelled to answer any question if it is considered by the Judge that the answer might incriminate the witness, or his or her husband or wife.
4. *Written, or documentary evidence*. When given in evidence the contents of a document must generally be proved by producing the original document and not an extract or a copy. Secondary evidence of the contents may be admitted

100

only in certain circumstances, as when the original document has been destroyed or cannot be produced.

5. *Confessions.* A confession is 'an admission made at any time by a person charged with a crime stating or suggesting the inference that he committed that crime. Confessions, if voluntary, are deemed to be relevant fact as against the persons who made them only' (Mr. Justice Stephen). To be admitted as evidence in a court of justice, it must be established that a confession is voluntary, and not made as a result of a threat, promise or inducement of any kind.

6. *Hearsay testimony.* Hearsay testimony is not admitted as evidence in a court of justice except in special cases, such as: (a) Admissions concerning a point at issue made by agents or others who are jointly interested with one of the parties to the action. But admissions clearly stated to be made '*without prejudice*' cannot be accepted as evidence in English law. (b) Declarations of deceased persons, made under certain circumstances (as while under the apprehension of immediate death) or regarding particular matters, such as rights of way, questions of pedigree, contents of will, etc.

7. *Circumstantial evidence.* Evidence that gives rise to the presumption of an occurrence, by proving circumstances that are usually or necessarily associated with events of a particular kind. Circumstantial evidence is thus distinguished from direct evidence which gives positive proof.

Logic
8. *Demonstrative evidence.* That which makes it evident to the mind that a proposition is true. Mathematical deductions give an example of demonstrative evidence, which is generally limited to proving that a conclusion necessarily follows from a particular set of premises and axioms. Demonstrative evidence is taken to be convincing as proof to any person of adequate intelligence: it is thus distinguished from *probable evidence*, which admits of varying degrees of probability.

Science
9. Observations, ascertained facts and principles cited for or against any given conclusion. Evidence is used in scientific

101

work less to give formal 'proof' of propositions than to establish probabilities. The various classes of evidence that are commonly recognized include (a) descriptive data (b) experimental evidence and (c) derived principles. Scientific measurements and other observations which are independent of the observer are classed as *objective evidence*. *Subjective evidence*, which depends on an evaluation made by the observer, is less reliable than objective evidence, since it is liable to observer errors of various kinds. By applying appropriate statistical methods it is sometimes possible to express probabilities in quantitative terms: evidence obtained in this way is known as *statistical evidence*.

In considering scientific evidence of any kind it is necessary to distinguish carefully between ascertained facts, established principles, and hypotheses. Scientific evidence must also conform to the rules of logic: failure to observe this may give rise to errors such as the common *post hoc ergo propter hoc* fallacy.

Comparative Religion
10. The word is used in a special sense for the various arguments given in support of Christianity and proofs given for the existence of a God. Such evidence includes (a) passages in the scriptures, (b) prophesies, (c) reports of events attributed to divine intervention, such as miracles and (d) opinions and convictions expressed by ecclesiastical authorities and others believed to be divinely inspired. The arguments are sometimes described collectively as 'the Evidences'.

EXISTENTIALISM

A doctrine developed by J. P. Sartre and others about 1935–1940. The basic teaching is that a person creates his own essential nature by the particular choices he makes. 'Man first exists, only afterwards is he this or that. Man has to create his own essence.' 'When we say that man chooses himself, we do mean that every one of us must choose himself.' 'To exercise his freedom of choice is a man's privilege and responsibility.' 'Man gains his self, his personality, in his decisions.' Existentialism teaches that people should recognize and face up to all the realities of life, instead of trying to conceal unpleasant facts or take refuge in irrational faiths and creeds.

In teaching the acceptance of the more sordid facts of life as an essential fact of existence, existentialism seeks to avoid disillusionment and to correct indulgence in over-optimistic hopes of the rapid reformation of the world. At its best, existentialism teaches a rational and realistic approach to life which may serve as a shield against false ideologies of every kind; but its critics claim that it promotes a pessimistic denial of progress, a morbid preoccupation with the pathological and an attitude of irresponsible complacency in the face of evil. While Sartre regarded reason as the main guide in a man's exercise of his freedom of choice, Kierkegaard developed the view that feelings, intuitions and passions should also operate in determining a person's choice. Existentialism may be regarded as a reaction from the many conflicting religious and political ideologies current in the period leading up to the Second World War of 1939–1945.

EXPLANATION

Common Language
'Explain' comes from the Latin *explanare*, to make plain. The word 'explanation' is used loosely in several different senses for (a) the process of explaining, (b) any fact that makes clear or accounts for an event, and (c) a statement that makes an event, object or procedure intelligible by relating it to other objects or facts known to the hearer.

An explanation is generally intended to answer the question How? or Why? in terms that the hearer or reader can understand. It may include a description of the causes and the sequence of changes leading up to an event: but an explanation differs from a description in that it generally includes an *evaluation* of the significance of the causal factors described. In the Common Language an explanation is often taken to mean a *justification* of an act.

Since an explanation must be expressed in terms that are meaningful to the hearer for whom it is intended, the terms of explanation should be appropriate for the age, education, experience, intelligence and understanding of the hearer. People living in primitive societies generally find it easier to understand explanations of natural events in personal (anthropomorphic) or supernatural terms, while in more developed societies the scientific explanations are generally preferred. The following classes of explanations may be distinguished:

1. *Anthropomorphic*. Events of any kind are explained in terms of the feelings, emotions and values of human beings. E.g. a ship is wrecked because the sea is angry.

(a) *Purposive*. The behaviour of animals and men is explained in terms of motives and purposes that are believed to determine their behaviour through the operation of free-will.

2. *Supernatural*. Events are attributed to the intervention of God or to the agency of supernatural spirits or to magic. E.g. the rain has come because the farmer prayed to God for rain.

(a) *Astrological*. Events are explained in terms of the movements of the stars and planets, which are held to influence human affairs by supernatural means. E.g. a child is sickly because her horoscope is unfavourable.

3. *Symbolic*. Events are explained by the use of metaphors, parables or other symbolic devices. The explanation of natural events given in myths, legends and in the holy scriptures are commonly believed to be symbolic.

4. *Causal*. This class of explanation, which is used in nearly all scientific work, treats events as a necessary result of the pre-existing material conditions. Events are explained in terms of the antecedent causes which lead up to them logically in accordance with natural laws. A causal explanation may include the definition of the relation between cause and effect in mathematical terms.

(a) *Deterministic*. Explanations of human and animal behaviour in causal terms are known as deterministic, since they preclude the possibility of freedom of choice or free will.

(b) *Mechanistic.* Explanation of behaviour in which living organisms are regarded as 'machines' in which the relation between cause and effect is of a strictly physicochemical kind.

5. *Explanatory models.* A model that represents the relation between cause and effect can serve as an explanation of a process or event. E.g. a model employing a mechanical pump can serve to explain the action of the heart, or a system of electronic valves to explain the action of the brain.

FAITH

Common Language
1. 'Faith' comes from the Latin *fidere*, to trust. To have faith in anything means to have confidence in it, or to rely on it. In this sense faith means confidence, reliance or trust (e.g. to have faith in God, or in humanity, or in an Order of Nature).
2. Adherence to a belief that cannot be justified by logical evidence. Belief that is based, not on reason and intellect, but on irrational conviction, generally for emotional reasons. Thus faith in immortality may be inspired by the fear of death.

Theology
3. Belief in a religious doctrine proceeding from reliance on the testimony of the scriptures (the Talmud, Holy Bible, Koran, etc) or from the authority of a Church (Christian, Mohammedan, Jewish, etc).
4. Conviction attributed to spiritual apprehension or supernatural illumination, through the exercise of a special human faculty.
5. A set of religious doctrines that should be believed. For example, the Mohammedan, Christian or Protestant faith.
6. Some religious writers use the word 'faith' in a sense which emphasizes the emotional aspect of religious beliefs, and regards faith as a kind of motive power. In this sense faith has been defined as 'the state of being ultimately concerned' (Tillich) in God, or in any other object of faith.

FIXTURE

Law

Fixtures are things added to houses or land which on addition immediately become part of the whole property.

The definition of 'fixtures' is a question that often arises in connexion with the sale or tenancy of houses, factories, offices and land. At the end of a tenancy a tenant is generally permitted to remove 'fittings', but not 'fixtures' and this is a common cause of dispute. There is no ready way of distinguishing between fixtures and fittings, but in general an article is a fixture if

(a) its removal would cause substantial damage to the property, or

(b) if intended as a permanent improvement of buildings or land.

Fixtures are generally taken to include doors, windows, locks and keys, mantelpieces, sinks, central heating equipment and articles cemented to walls or floors: also trees and garden shrubs.

Fittings have been taken to include electric fires, light brackets, fire grates, cooking stoves, window-blinds, curtain-rods, pictures, mirrors, splash-backs, stair-carpet fittings, electrical immersion heaters and articles screwed to walls or floors, provided always that (a) they can be removed without doing substantial damage and that (b) they have not been substituted for fixtures belonging to the landlord. However, it is hard to make general rules; thus mantelpieces are generally accepted as fixtures, but in some cases ornamental chimney-pieces have been held to be fittings.

In some cases it is necessary to distinguish between *landlord's fixtures* and *tenant's fixtures*. A tenant's fixtures generally include articles or equipment affixed to the premises of a tenant for the purpose of his profession or trade. Thus, at the end of a tenancy a nurseryman may remove his greenhouse, and also small trees or shrubs that he has planted. A tenant must remove his fixtures before his tenancy expires, for whatever remains on the premises when the landlord resumes possession is legally the landlord's property. If a tenant has replaced a landlord's

106

fixture by another fixture, the tenant may not remove his own fixture unless he replaces it by the landlord's fixture or by a similar one.

A tenant farmer has the statutory right to remove fixtures, which include any engines, machinery, fencing, or other fixtures affixed to a holding by the tenant, and also certain buildings erected by him, provided that he observes certain obligations. Thus, before he may remove any fixture or building, the tenant must pay all rent owing by him and satisfy all other obligations to the landlord in respect of the holding. He must also give one month's notice of his intention before removing any fixture or building from the holding.

FREQUENCY

Common Language
1. Coming from the Latin *frequens*, meaning crowded, 'frequency' is used in the common language to mean the fact of recurring often at short intervals.
2. The frequency of a recurrent phenomenon is the number of occurrences in a unit period of time.

Physics
3. In a continuous cyclical or periodic phenomenon the frequency is the rate of recurrence, or in c.g.s. units the number of cycles per second. In other words, frequency is the reciprocal of the period (which is the time required for one complete cycle).

The frequency is commonly used to characterize wave motion, such as sound, light, X-rays and wireless waves, and in electricity to express the rate of alteration of an alternating electric current. The word 'frequency' should not be applied, in this sense of the word, to any recurrent phenomenon which is not strictly periodic.

Statistics
4. The frequency is the number of times a given phenomenon occurs in a specified sample or population. Thus the number of individuals with a particular score of a variable

such as age or height is the frequency of the score in the population. The number of cases coming into any particular class is the class frequency.

The arrangement of figures giving the numbers of cases of any variable falling within class intervals arranged in order of magnitude (such as age or height) is called the *frequency distribution*. The figures may be arranged systematically to give a *frequency table*, or plotted graphically to give a *frequency polygon* or *frequency curve*. The *normal frequency curve* (or Gaussian curve) is a symmetrical bell-shaped curve giving the frequency of different values of a variable when the deviation of individual values from the mean is subject to chance, or varies according to laws of probability.

5. For some purposes the frequency is defined as the ratio of actual occurrences to the maximum possible number of occurrences of an event.

Medicine
6. The word 'frequency' is used in medicine in sense (1) of the Common Language in contexts as, for example, the statement that a patient is suffering from 'frequency of micturition'.

The word is also used in sense (2) in contexts such as: 'The frequency of the pulse is seventy-eight a minute.'

FRUSTRATION

Common Language
1. An emotional reaction to failure to attain an objective. It is characterized by feelings of anger, irritation and impatience, often with phases of depression over lack of success and anxiety over the implied threat to self-esteem. Besides the subjective feelings, frustration is associated with objective signs of emotional stress.

2. The word 'frustration' is used also for the *situation* or *condition* of a person experiencing considerable difficulty in attaining a goal and for (3) the *act* of frustrating, (preventing some objective to be attained.)

Psychology

4. Frustration is a part of the normal experience of all goal-seeking organisms, and in the higher animals it plays an important part in their development and maturation. The normal healthy reaction of the mature individual to failure is an orderly change of plans, with the abandonment of former objectives and the redefinition of new and attainable goals. In that way the situation is mastered and the sense of frustration overcome. The immature individual reacts characteristically with disorganized behaviour (tantrums, sulking or self-pity) but he may nevertheless learn from the experience. Conditions for optimal development depend on the individual, but generally they require that neither success nor failure should prevail in excessive degree.

While periods of frustration are the normal experience, unduly prolonged frustration must be regarded as generally undesirable in view of the stress involved. The manifestations of frustration are pathological in the over-protected individual who has failed to mature and in whom an immature type of frustration persists into adult life. Excessive or prolonged frustration may lead to the development of neurotic symptoms and a pathological disorganization of the personality.

Psychoanalysis

5. Freud (1911) regarded frustration as one of the main factors leading to the development of a sense of reality in the young infant. The infant finds that certain sources of gratification, such as milk from the breast, can be absent as well as present, and so he learns that the world contains important classes of things outside itself that are impermanent. Excessive deprivation during the period of maturation increases the strength of the id impulses (drives) and may lead to a failure in the development of ego functions. The ego is therefore unable to perform its proper task of mediating between the id and the environment, so that the individual is unable to make the best use of all the opportunities for enjoyment that the environment can provide.

FUNCTION. FUNCTIONALISM. FUNCTIONAL

Common Language

1. Performance, operation or activity in general (from the Latin *fungere*, to perform).
2. The special activity or role in which anything fulfils its proper purpose. Thus we can talk of the functions of a machine, of a building, or of an individual of a particular class, such as a policeman. In this sense of the word 'functional' means serving its specific purpose.
3. A social ceremony or performance, generally of an official kind, e.g. a banquet or a presentation.

Mathematics

4. A variable quantity the value of which is determined by one or more other variables. Thus if for example $y = \log x$, we can say that the dependent variable y is a function of the independent variable x. The relation may be expressed as $y = f(x)$.

The word is used in this sense in the term *functional analysis*, a method of scientific investigation in which the conditions determining an event are studied by systematically modifying the conditions.

Biology

5. The specific biological role or use of a cell, structure, organ or organism.
6. The activity of an organ, structure, cell, etc. in which it fulfils its biological role. Thus the function of a muscle may be defined in terms of the work performed, the function of the kidneys in chemical terms and the functions of the brain in psychological terms. The state of the organ during functional activity may be distinguished from that of the organ while at rest. In this context the meaning of the word is usually restricted to the major biological activity of the organ, and function may be distinguished from associated electrical, metabolic and other phenomena: but the word is also used in a wider sense in which associated electrical, structural and metabolic changes are all included as part of the function.

Psychology
7. The term *functional psychology* or *functionalism* was given to the study of mental phenomena as dynamic processes serving a biological function in relation to the life of the individual. This viewpoint, developed by Stumpf, Angell, Dewey and others, differs from that of earlier psychologists who were concerned primarily with studying the content of consciousness or with descriptions of the 'mind' in more static terms.

Medicine
8. The term *functional* is used to describe disorders due to the dysfunction of an organ rather than to a structural change or lesion. E.g. functional deafness.

Psychiatry
9. The term 'functional' is commonly applied in psychiatry to psychoses and other forms of mental disorder that cannot be attributed to any known structural or biochemical abnormality of the brain and must therefore be described in behavioural terms. Examples are the schizophrenias and manic-depressive psychoses. The functional psychoses are thus distinguished from the so-called 'organic' psychoses, in which there is a demonstrable lesion of the brain.

This use of the word 'functional' has been criticized since, strictly speaking, structure and function are interdependent: no biological process can occur without change of structure, and whenever the brain functions there is organic change. In this context 'functional' carries the implication that a mental disorder so described is due to psychological rather than to physical causes: but here again the term may be misleading. Thus, general paresis was classed as a functional psychosis before the discovery of the spirochaete, and further improvements in pathological technique might necessitate the reclassification of other so-called 'functional' psychoses. In view of these difficulties many psychiatrists use the word *psychogenic* for conditions attributed to psychological causes, and prefer to avoid the use of the word 'functional' in this sense.

Art

10. The practical use, role or purpose of any building, structure, vehicle, piece of furniture or other article designed for practical use. In this sense of the word, 'functional' means serving a practical purpose. Functional structures, etc. are thus distinguished from those that are ornamental.

11. The term *functionalism* has been given to a teaching, and to a derived style of architectural and interior design, developed about 1920–1930. The leading principle is the achievement of fitness for purpose by the direct use of the available materials. This style of design tends to avoid unnecessary ornament, and particularly the incorporation of non-functional features of older styles, which serve no practical purpose (as, for example, the use of grecian pillars or half-timbering in a modern building made of concrete and steel). Examples of good functional design are to be found in tubular steel furniture, streamlined automobiles, aircraft and in many industrial and other buildings such as those designed by the architects Le Corbusier and Gropius. In this sense of the word 'functional' means designed in such a way as to express fitness for purpose.

GENETIC

Common language

'Genetic' can mean (1) relating to *origins* and development, but it is now generally taken to mean (2) relating to *inheritance*. In this sense of the word the genetic constitution of an individual determines the physical and mental characteristics inherited from the parents, and which may be passed on from one generation to another. The genetic endowment is fixed at the time of fertilisation of the ovum, and is in the genes which transmit hereditary factors of a physical and mental kind.

Biology

'Genetic' means relating to heredity and evolution, or to the genes which determine the inherited characteristics of plants and animals, and are the units making up the genetic

112

code. A gene is part of the chromosomes which are present in every living cell in the body. In man each cell contains two sets of twenty-four chromosomes (one set from each parent) or forty-eight altogether, and each chromosome carries about 1,000 genes. The genes, which are nucleo-protein (DNA) structures, are believed to operate by controlling the synthesis of enzymes which determine the metabolic characteristics of the cells. The activity of a gene depends on its environment, and environmental factors therefore play a part in the development of the hereditary pattern corresponding to the genetic constitution.

GOD

Common Language
In every civilization the idea of God has undergone slow, progressive changes. The gods of primitive peoples were mostly conceived as cruel, brutal superhuman beings, who demanded human sacrifices and other savage rights. But from the earliest times there have been groups of enlightened individuals who have striven for the accept-ance of views that are more enlightened and more humane. Thus the primitive gods of the earlier Greeks became gradually purified of their blood-lust and replaced by the more elevated gods and goddesses of Olympus; and these personal gods in human form, with their cults and mysteries, gradually became credited with moral virtues. Later the Olympian gods were in turn rejected by the more enlightened of the Greeks, or accepted only as symbols of the spiritual forces that sway the destinies of men. Thus Zeus, originally a personal god, who punished his enemies with thunderbolts and to whom sacrifices were made, was described by later Greek writers in abstract terms as 'day-night, summer-winter, war-peace, satiety-hunger' (Heraclitus) and again as 'all-seeing, all-hearing, and all-minded' (Xenophanes).

A similar progression can be seen from the primitive God of the Old Testament who demanded the sacrifice of Isaac and enjoyed the 'sweet savour' of burning flesh, through the more advanced concepts of God held by Job and Micah, to

113

the merciful God of Love conceived by Jesus of Nazareth.

At the present time many different concepts of God are held, while at the same time remnants of the old primitive ideas still survive in some parts of the world. In some primitive societies men such as King Darius, Alexander and the Ptolomies have been worshipped as gods, and until recent times there have been people who credited divinity to the Emperor of Japan, to the Aga Khan and to the Holy Father. There are still many Moslems and Christians who believe that God intervenes personally in the individual affairs of men by performing miracles and by similar supernatural acts. They regard God as a paternal figure who takes an individual interest in every human being in the world and who can be prayed to for personal guidance and help. Others believe that God holds over men the threat of a Day of Judgement, when sinners will be made to suffer eternally in the tortures of hell. Some think of God as a *Creator* who made the world, arguing that since the world exists, somebody must have made it, and hence there is a God: 'An all-seeing, all-good, all-powerful Father in heaven'.

Some use the word 'God' as symbolizing an impersonal *principle*, of goodness, beauty and perfection in the world, a god that has no material or spiritual existence, but exists only in men's minds as an abstract concept symbolizing qualities such as goodness, love etc. Others believe that the will of God is revealed to men through their consciences. Mahatma Gandhi, who described God as 'Absolute Truth', admitted that he had never found God, but added that he was still seeking Him. There are many today who completely reject the idea of a God and according to recent figures a high proportion of those leaving schools in England and America are agnostics who are not convinced of God's existence. 'I cannot conceive of a God who rewards and punishes his creatures. An individual who could survive his physical death is also beyond my comprehension, nor do I wish it otherwise: such notions are for the fears or absurd egoism of feeble souls' (Albert Einstein). One of the greatest religions of the world, Buddhism, has risen to great moral and intellectual heights without using the idea of God at all; in place of God it has Dharma, the

Eternal Law. Perhaps this is not so far removed from Aristotle's concept of God as the Prime Mover.

It is evident that the word 'God' stands for a great many different concepts in men's minds, and many people have no clear idea of what they mean by it. Yet the idea of a God expresses something that has been a help and an inspiration to many, and especially to those suffering hardships and in need. Thus in the words of the Rabbi Ben Ezra, 'All that I could never be, all that men despised in me – that am I to God.' It expresses something that is not easily put into words, but as put by Voltaire, 'If there were no God we should need to invent one.'

Law

An Act of God (*Damnum fatale*) is an event due to natural causes and not to any human agency, and which could not have been forseen or provided against by reasonable care. Provision is commonly made in insurance and other types of agreement for Acts of God, which include for example damage by lightning or by earthquake. The Courts have held that the sudden death of a motorist, by a heart attack, is an Act of God; but in some cases they have held that damage due to exceptionally heavy rain, or to an exceptionally high tide is not so caused. The term 'Act of God' derives from the belief that was commonly held in earlier times that inexplicable disasters were inflicted by God as a punishment for wrong-doing.

GOOD

Common Language

'Good' can mean (1) enjoyable or giving satisfaction, as in 'a good breakfast', 'a good time'. It can mean (2) well-made, appropriate or serviceable for some specific purpose as in 'a good fit', 'good agreement', 'a good recipe'. It can mean (3) sound or genuine, as in 'a good egg'. When referring to persons 'good' can mean (4) skilful or competent, as in 'a good teacher', 'a good dancer'. It can mean (5) well-behaved and dutiful, a 'good servant', 'a good child'. It can mean (6) kind, considerate, charitable and benevolent, as in 'a good friend'.

'Good' is also used to mean (7) conformity to a code of behaviour which is that of a specific organization or group, as in 'a good Christian', 'a good Socialist', 'a good American'.

When used as a noun 'good' is the opposite of 'evil', but individual judgements differ over what is held to be good. The definition of good and evil is a problem that has been considered by wise men and philosophers down through the ages, and different answers have been given by different adherents to different religious creeds. Since we have no absolute standard or ultimate criterion to which we can refer, the meaning of the word 'good' is not clear unless the relevant code of belief is specified.

GOVERNMENT

Common Language
A government is an organized body of persons engaged in directing the affairs of a country by establishing laws, directing the administration and exercising control through the army and police. Montesquieu developed the doctrine of the Separation of Powers, according to which only legislature should make laws, only the Judges judge and only the executive administrate. This form of safeguard is incorporated in the American constitution; but in England the same ministers who direct the law-making in Parliament are also responsible for the administration. The governments freely chosen and elected by the people in democratic states differ widely from the governments of dictatorships or 'police states', which keep the legislation in the hands of a few who are primarily concerned with maintaining their own power and who restrict the liberties of the people, insisting for example that the individual has no right to leave the country or to criticise the government. (See *CAPITALISM, COMMUNISM*)

GUARANTEE. GUARANTY

Common Language
A guarantee (sometimes spelt 'guaranty') is a written undertaking or promise to perform some undertaking, such

116

as the fulfilment of an agreement, the supply of satisfactory equipment, or the payment of a debt. Since a written guarantee is legally binding, it can be an asset for the purchaser when buying something such as new equipment or a new car, to receive a guarantee giving the right to demand that the maker should remedy any defects or replace any faulty parts. A guarantee must generally be signed by the purchaser and returned to the maker. It is not always appreciated that the guarantee forms issued by some firms include clauses making the manufacturer the sole judge of the strength of any claim, or releasing the manufacturer from liability for the consequences of any negligence. Under those conditions significant benefits may be lost and the nature of the guarantee is changed.

HEALTH

Common Language
Health is (1) the degree of physical and mental fitness of an individual or a community, the extent of soundness in body and mind. Health can also mean (2) complete physical and mental well-being, free from illness of any kind. A person can wish to have 'health and happiness'. Health is (3) a toast drunk as a sign of respect, or to express a wish for the well-being of a person or an institution.

Medicine
'Health' is defined in the constitution of the World Health Organisation as (4) 'a state of complete physical, mental and social well-being and not merely the absence of disease or infirmity'. This definition has been criticised on the grounds that, since nobody is in a state of complete physical, mental and social well-being, it could imply that everyone is sick. An alternative definition is (5) a normal state of body and mind, with all parts functioning normally.

Mental health is a relatively enduring state of good psychological adjustment in which a person is achieving self-realisation, has a zest for living and is able to maintain harmonious relations with other people. Freud defined mental health as 'ability to love and ability to work'.

HUMANISM

Common Language

The humanist movement started in Europe in the four-
teenth century at a time when learning, which was then
almost entirely in the hands of the priests and monks, was
largely restricted to theology. The original humanists were
the literary men of the classical Renaissance who rebelled
against the narrow outlook of the mediaeval divines.
Instead of limiting their studies to the 'sacred' literature,
they directed their attention instead to the cultural achieve-
ments of men as poets, writers, scientists and philosophers.
Their studies led to the rediscovery of the classical Greek
and Roman poets and philosophers whose work had been
neglected during the mediaeval period.

Many of the early humanists, such as Erasmus and
Thomas More were sincere Christians; but because of their
opposition to the monopoly of learning by the theologians,
and their admiration for the pagan literature of Greece and
Rome, they were regarded with suspicion as 'materialists'
by more orthodox members of the Church. Humanism, in
the original sense of the word, thus meant (1) the
intellectual movement and general outlook which laid
emphasis on the study of all aspects of human culture and
especially the revival of classical learning led by the
scholars of the Renaissance.

With the advance of humanist studies in the universities
there began the early development of science and the
growth of scientific scepticism. The humanists came to
include a number who rejected belief in divine revelation or
in the authority of the Scriptures, while the Church was
seen by many as a force opposed to progress and enlightenment. The term *humanism* then came to mean (2) the
teachings and beliefs of the free-thinkers, secularists,
agnostics, rationalists and others who joined forces in the
humanist movement directed at that time mainly against
the dogma and authoritarian teachings of the Christian
Church. This negative, anti-theistic concept of humanism
has continued until recent times.

Humanism is currently understood as (3) a system of
beliefs based, not on divine revelation, but on human

reason and understanding. The ethical and moral aspects of humanism are similar in general to those of the Christian community in which humanism has developed, but the humanist movement is not authoritarian in nature; it is essentially tolerant in respecting individual human values and beliefs which are sincerely held. There is no orthodoxy of humanism, since it is a basic tenet that every person should be free to think things out for himself and work out his own principles. According to one definition humanism is 'the outlook on the world which respects man as bearer of a fundamental responsibility for his attitude and his conduct, without relying on the guidance of a revelation or on the help of supernatural powers' (First International Congress on Humanism and Ethical Culture, 1952).

In its positive aspects modern humanism is characterized by the belief that effort should be directed towards the deliberate rational quest for human welfare. Emphasis is laid on the worthwhileness of certain ways of living, such as those involved in the practical aim of serving humanity and 'making the world a better place to live in'. While supporting every kind of activity deriving from the exercise of social conscience, modern humanism still retains the original humanist concern for furthering the higher cultural aspirations of man in poetry, music, science, philosophy and the arts.

There are humanist philosophies (such as Positivism, Existentialism, Phenomenalism), but one cannot speak of *the* philosophy of humanism. Humanism is not a *specific* philosophy or religion, but rather a cultural tradition which has gradually evolved in the course of time, a wide stream of thought which, flowing within certain limits, is defined by certain central affirmations and rejections. A basic affirmation is that knowledge can be acquired only by a combination of observation and reason: rejected are belief in divine revelation, visions and all supernatural powers.

HUMOUR

Common Language
1. Humour is the quality of a situation or behaviour which

excites amusement and laughter, as in a conversation, a picture, a writing or a play. It may depend on suggestions which are ridiculous, comical, joking, extravagant or absurd, and not intended to be taken seriously. Humour is the leading theme of the branch of drama known as *comedy*, in which characters speaking the language of everyday life cause amusement, usually by the introduction of an element of exaggeration or caricature, which can make a mockery of accepted standards. In *farce* the humour is of a more extravagant and boisterous kind, as when characters normally expected to behave with dignity are depicted as behaving like naughty children. A farce can arouse laughter, merriment, hilarity and mirth. *Wit* is a type of humour at a more intellectual level, depending on the perception of subtle relations between ideas which are not normally associated. This may be expressed in a neat and pointed way, causing pleasant surprise and amusement in the hearer (unless he is the one against whom the wit is directed).

2. In another sense of the word humour is the state of mind, temperament or mental disposition of a person who can be in a good humour (cheerful and kind) or a bad humour (irritable and mean) at different times.

Anatomy
3. A humour is the fluid or semi-fluid content of certain organs of the body, such as the *vitreous humour* of the eye. which fills the posterior chamber behind the lens. The liquid humours of the body were formerly believed to determine a person's temperament and mental disposition. Hence the expressions 'sanguine', 'choleric', 'phlegmatic' and 'melancholic'.

HYSTERIA

Common Language
1. A display of excessive or unnatural emotional behaviour, as in tantrums of rage, in uncontrolled weeping, in screaming with anxiety, or in the excesses of an agitated mob. The word is also used in the plural, *hysterics*, for outbursts of uncontrolled laughter or crying.

Psychiatry
2. The meaning of the word in psychiatry is different from
that in the Common Language. Hysteria is a form of mental
disorder characterized by physical symptoms, or a disturbance of behaviour, not attributable to direct physical
causes. Hysterical symptoms may mimic any form of
physical illness: they include headaches, fainting, stammer-
ing, mutism, nervous tics, paralyses, contractures, anaes-
thesias, fits, vomiting, deafness, blindness, loss of memory,
fugues, bed-wetting, suicidal gestures, 'making scenes', lack
of appetite, breathlessness and palpitations. Hysteria may
occur as a reaction to stress or conflict, and the hysterical
symptoms are generally of a kind that confer an advantage
by providing a means of escape from anxiety, from
responsibility or from an unpleasant situation: thus a
headache may prevent attendance at an examination. But it
is characteristic of hysteria that the symptoms are involuntary and the hysteric is not aware of any motive for them:
hysteria differs in this respect from malingering. The failure
to admit to conscious awareness certain unacceptable
aspects of behaviour implies a disturbance of the normal
integrating mechanisms of the central nervous system: this
is sometimes described as 'dissociation'. Thus the hysteric
is able to exhibit purposeful, integrated behaviour and also
unintegrated behaviour (incongruous hysterical symptoms)
at the same time. The tendency of a person of hysterical
personality to react to a stressful situation by forms of
behaviour that are dissociated from the other functions of
the personality may be regarded as a form of immaturity,
since a lack of integration of this kind is relatively common
in the young child. Hysteria is more common in women
than in men, and the word 'hysteria' derives from the Greek
husterikós, 'pertaining to the womb', since the womb was
believed in ancient times to be the seat of the disorder.
   A condition in which hysterical symptoms of a bodily
kind result directly from mental conflict or anxiety, with a
diminution of overt emotion, is described as *conversion
hysteria*. A person of hysterical personality may tend to
exaggerate the symptoms of a physical illness or injury and
so develop a *hysterical overlay*. The tendency to exaggerate
the extent of an injury may be especially marked when a

question of compensation arises: the condition is then known as *compensation hysteria*.

Hysterical symptoms can often be removed by powerful suggestion, especially if given under hypnosis: but this does not remove the underlying conflict, so that if one symptom is removed in this way another may take its place. The dramatic removal by suggestion of hysterical symptoms such as blindness or paralysis is probably the basis of many alleged 'miraculous cures'.

IMMUNITY

Common Language
1. Immunity means exemption from, or freedom from, anything injurious.

Law
2. Immunity means exemption from a legal obligation, duty or liability.

Biology
3. Immunity means freedom, in some degree, from liability to infection, or to injury from a toxic substance. *Natural* immunity is the inborn power to resist injury from infectious or toxic substances: it depends on a complex system of defence mechanisms. Factors concerned in resistance to infection include (a) local inflammatory reaction, (b) removal of foreign bodies by phagocytes, (c) production of anti-bodies by cells of the reticuloendothelial system, (d) liberation of interferon by cells invaded by a virus and (e) factors affecting the permeability of the tissues.
4. *Acquired* immunity is an acquired resistance to a particular type of infection. Immunity may be acquired (a) by an attack of a disease, or (b) by repeated exposure to small doses of infection, (c) in an infant, by taking up protective substances from the mother's milk or (d) by treatments such as vaccination or injection of antibodies from an immune animal or person, which gives immunity by artificial means.

5. *Immunology* is the branch of medical science which deals with the defence mechanisms of the body against foreign agents such as AIDS and other infectious organisms and poisons. It deals with the study of the resistance of human beings and animals to viruses, parasites, bacteria and the toxins produced by them. Important aspects of immunology are (a) the study of mechanisms by which cells produce antibodies that react with foreign agents, (b) the control of infectious diseases by means of vaccines which give immunity, (c) the study of the reactions of the body to transplanted organs and to cancer cells and (d) the study of hypersensitivity of the body to substances containing specific chemical groups.

IMPOTENCE

Common Language
1. Powerlessness, helplessness, lack of power to act (due to external circumstances).
2. Lack of strength, feebleness, incapacity.
3. Incapacity for sexual intercourse in the male.

Medicine
4. Impotence is a symptom found in a number of different conditions characterized by incapacity for sexual intercourse. The word was formerly applied in a wide sense to the lack of reproductive capacity, either in the male or in the female: but the meaning of the word is now generally restricted to the inability of the male to perform the functions of the male in copulating with the female. Impotence may imply:
    (a) inability to be sexually aroused by the opposite sex,
    (b) incapacity to achieve or maintain an erection of the penis, adequate for copulation when sexually aroused,
    (c) incapacity to ejaculate semen during copulation (when sexually aroused and in erection).
Impotence may be complete, or relative and dependent on the circumstances. Thus it may be invariable or limited to conditions of anxiety, stress or fatigue. It may be caused by physical factors, such as a lesion of the spinal cord

(atonic impotence) or an endocrine imbalance. Impotence of endocrine origin is a common symptom of the male climacteric in middle age.

Impotence may also be caused by psychological factors such as anxiety, tension, or depression. This form of impotence is frequently associated with premature ejaculation; the reason for this is that adrenaline, which is released in anxiety, inhibits erection of the penis, but makes the seminal vesicles contract. Hysterical impotence is a form of neurosis that may be due to an underlying mental conflict.

Law
6. Impotence is defined as the physical inability of a man or woman to perform the act of sexual intercourse. Incurable impotence lasting from the time of marriage makes the marriage contract no longer binding: the marriage can be declared null and void by bringing a suit of nullity of marriage.

INFLATION

Common Language
Inflation is (1) the act or process of blowing up or causing to swell out, as in inflating a tyre or a balloon. The word is now commonly used to cover (2) any form of general rise in costs and prices associated with a fall in the value of money. That occurs (a) if the money supply provided by the Government is increased faster than the goods and services which need to be financed, and that is known as 'true inflation'. A similar rise in costs and prices can also be caused by (b) an increase in the cost of imports such as oil or raw materials, or (c) by increases in wages and salaries. There are thus different forms of inflation due to different causes.

Economics
The amount of money issued in a country is normally just sufficient to enable the consumers to buy the goods available for purchase. Inflation is (3) the process (or condition) in which the purchasing power of the consumers exceeds the supply of goods, so that retail prices rise. It is

popularly expressed as 'too much money chasing too few goods'. Under these conditions the cost of living rises and the real value of money falls. The rise in prices creates a demand for higher wages; prices and wages thus tend to follow one another upwards in a 'price-wage spiral'. Employment tends to increase, in view of the increased demand for goods and the availability of money.

Inflation may be caused by a shortage of goods, or by an increase in the issue of money. If currency and credits are reduced, the opposite state of affairs, known as *deflation* is produced: wages and prices then fall and there tends to be unemployment.

There is no simple test that can show whether inflation is present or not. In a country free from monetary controls (i.e. in a state of 'free economy') a general rise in prices is the best indication of inflation. But prices are not an entirely satisfactory index of inflation, since prices of different kinds do not always move together in the same direction. Thus in the inflation of 1929, in England and the USA, security prices soared while basic material prices remained unchanged. Separate consideration must be given to (a) retail prices, (b) wholesale prices, (c) basic raw material (commodity) prices and (d) security prices. Another index of inflation is an increase in the velocity of circulation of money; this is shown by an increase in the clearance of cheques by the banks. Inflation is indicated also by an increase in bank deposits.

In a country where wages and prices are controlled or measures such as rationing are enforced, prices cannot rise as they would in a 'free economy'. Under such conditions the immediate inflationary effects of increasing the issue of money are prevented. The term *suppressed inflation* is used to describe this state of affairs, in which active inflation is prevented by controls, but would occur if the controls were lifted.

A slow *'creeping inflation'* due to the gradual rise of wages and prices in the 'price-wage spiral' may occur without the operation of the usual basic inflationary conditions of excessive spending and the creation of new credit to finance it. In most countries a slow progressive rise in wages and prices, and a corresponding fall in the value of money, has occurred throughout the whole course of history. The extent to which this change is reversible depends on current social attitudes and factors such as the influence of the trades unions.

INFORMATION

Common Language
1. This word was originally used only in a human context to mean what one person may tell another. In this sense information presupposes the existence of a human recipient for whom it has meaning as news, tidings, or intelligence. The word is now commonly used to describe facts that are relevant to a specific problem or situation and which can be communicated directly by word of mouth, by gesture, by letter or in the form of a code. Information can be stored in the memory, in books, in films and in other ways.

Law
2. Information is a statement made by an informer accusing another person of breaking the law: a complaint or charge made by an informer to a court or a magistrate in order to start legal proceedings against a person.
3. Information is a statement of fact made to the court by the attorney-general or another officer of the Crown in respect of a civil claim.

Biology
4. Information is a general term for any pattern of stimuli received by a living organism, which can influence behaviour by producing a characteristic response. Thus food-seeking, mating, defence and other activities of an animal are influenced by information received through sensory channels from the internal organs of the body, as well as from the outside world. In a general stimulus situation, information is the property of the stimuli which serves as a *cue*.
5. Genetic information is that which determines the genetic endowment of chemical and structural characteristics inherited by a living organism. Genetic information is

communicated from parents to offspring by nucleoprotein structures (chromosomes) contained in the nuclei of ovum and spermatozoon: it is communicated from one cell to another by the division of the chromosomes when a cell divides.

Communication Theory
6. Information is that which can produce a characteristic response when transmitted from one system to another.

Information Theory
7. Information is the property that enables some or all of the items of an ensemble to be classified into different categories. The greater the amount of information available, the smaller is the number of operations required for classification. The amount of information (H) in an ensemble varies inversely with the average number of steps required to classify the items. The unit measure of information is the *bit*, which is named from the first and last letters of '*binary digit*'. The *bit* is defined as the amount of information which, in a given system containing a known number of alternative events, reduces the alternatives by one half. The *bit* is always relative to the particular assemblage to which it refers: it bears no relation to the *bit* for any other system. The word 'information' is used in information theory to express quantitatively a property which is opposite to the degree of uncertainty or unexpectedness of events in a physical system. In this context the meaning of 'information' differs widely from that in the Common Language. Information about the complexity of form is expressed in terms of the *logon*, which is the unit of measure of structural information: the reliability of information is measured in terms of the *metron*, which is the unit of matrical information.

INSIGHT

Common Language
1. Comprehension of underlying truth or meaning; vision that penetrates beneath the surface.

Psychiatry

2. Awareness by a person who is mentally disordered of the true nature of his own mental state. Thus a patient is said to show insight into his condition at times when he shows complete or partial awareness of the irrationality of his delusions, obsessions, compulsions or disturbances of mood.

3. In psychoanalysis, insight is taken to mean the extent of a patient's true understanding of the origins and unconscious mechanisms of his behaviour.

4. A patient's own explanation (which may distorted, untrue or incomplete) of his mental disorder.

Psychology

5. The sudden grasp or apprehension of a relationship, meaning, significance or truth; e.g. apprehension of the relevance of an object for the solution of a problem.

It is generally recognized that insight plays an important part in learning, and learning by insight (e.g. by apprehending a method of solving a problem) is sometimes contrasted wuth the more primitive process of learning by trial-and-error. Some psychologists have believed that insight is largely attributable to a transfer of previous learning: Hebb regards insight as a particular operation of intelligence. In this sense of the word insight is a mental process; but the word is used also for (6) the mental capacity or faculty responsible for sudden apprehension and sometimes also for (7) that which is apprehended.

The sudden feeling of enlightenment or inspiration associated with insight has been described as the *a-ha!* experience.

8. The direct apprehension of form, meaning or truth, without the involvement of reasoning or memory.

INTELLIGENCE

Common Language

1. The word is used loosely in the Common Language for general intellectual capacity, cleverness, reasoning power,

sagacity, or quickness of understanding. Thus a person's intelligence may be judged from his or her quickness at learning, ability to pass examinations, ability to adapt to a novel situation, skill at solving a problem or ability to profit by experience. Intellectual capacity should not be confused with intellectual *ability*: thus a person of average intellectual capacity and intelligence may be idle and therefore have less than average ability. The word 'intelligence' is used both for the intellectual *capacity* described and also for (2) the mental *faculty* of understanding, or intellect.

3. The word is used in a different sense for communicated information or news, and particularly for information communicated to the army, navy or police.

Psychology

4. The nature of intelligence has been a subject of controversy for many years, and a number of different meanings have been given to the word. Some have regarded intelligence as a composite made up of a number of independent unitary capacities (Thorndike, 1903): others have believed it to be a general capacity underlying many different kinds of mental abilities in varying degrees (Spearman, 1904). Unitary types of intelligence that have been described include *abstract intelligence* (the capacity for dealing effectively with abstract concepts and symbols); *verbal intelligence* (the capacity for dealing effectively with verbal symbols); *mechanical or concrete intelligence* (the capacity to solve problems involving concrete objects); *social intelligence* (effectiveness in interpersonal relations); *academic intelligence* (capacity for utilizing academic instruction and learning from books) and *aesthetic intelligence* (capacity for evaluating aesthetic values). It is no longer commonly believed that these different forms of intelligence exist independently of each other as unitary traits, and such terms are therefore now less widely used. Others have regarded intelligence as divisible into vectors of intellectual capacity which include factors of perception, space visualisation, insight, verbal comprehension, verbal fluency, reaction speed, number facility, deduction, flexibility and judgement.

Halstead (1950) has differentiated between *biological*

intelligence, which bears directly upon the capacity of an organism for controlled adaptability, and *psychometric intelligence* which does not. Biological intelligence, which implies mental flexibility and versatility in adjusting to a situation, is biologically important for the survival of the organism. It can be separated by factorial analysis into four main dimensions: (a) the capacity for abstracting universals or true concepts, (b) cerebral power or intellectual drive, (c) a memory factor or capacity for organizing experience and (d) the capacity for relating behavioural response to the situation perceived.

Hebb has distinguished between three divergent concepts of intelligence. *Intelligence A* is 'an innate potential, the capacity for development, a fully innate property that amounts to the possession of a good brain and a good neural metabolism'. *Intelligence B* is 'the functioning of a brain in which development has gone on in a 'completely stimulating environment', remembering that some environments are more facilitating and stimulating than others'. *Intelligence C* is 'the result of the individual's intelligence-test score – i.e. the result of an attempt to assess intelligence B'.

Intelligence in man has sometimes been defined in such terms as 'the ability to think in abstract terms' (Terman): but definitions of this kind are of limited applicability and it may be noted that they cannot easily be applied to animals. It may be doubted in any case whether intelligence in an animal should be regarded as qualitatively similar to that in man. By most tests the most intelligent animal is of lower intelligence than a mentally defective child.

Current concepts of intelligence thus differ mainly in respect of (a) the comprehensiveness of the concept, (b) the extent to which it is regarded as innate or experimental and (c) the extent to which it is identified with psychometric values. The following definitions may be useful in illustrating some of the different meanings given to the word:

5. Intelligence is the ability to comprehend complex relationships and adapt effectively to novel situations in seeking a goal.

This may be compared with a definition of intelligence by G Stoddard as 'the ability to undertake activities that are characterized by difficulty, complexity, abstractness, economy, adaptiveness to a goal, social value, and the emergence of originals'. Intelligence of this kind is largely a product of experience and clearly it depends to a large extent on the environment in which development has taken place.

6. Intelligence is the innate potential capacity for comprehending complex relationships and adapting effectively in seeking a goal.

According to this concept of intelligence it depends on the structural and metabolic characteristics of the brain and the whole hereditary constitution of the individual. It is independent of education, environment and experience, and not affected by age.

7. Intelligence is that which is measured by a specified intelligence test.

A number of tests involving problem solving, arithmetical computation, completion of verbal relations, and other intellectual tasks have been devised for measuring intelligence; but the scores obtained with different tests do not generally agree and it is difficult to be sure what exactly is measured by them. Different tests may relate particularly to (a) inborn or innate intelligence, (b) abilities acquired through experience, (c) a general factor (Spearman's G) regarded as common to all tests of ability, or (d) more specific abilities. Verbal tests require a facility in the use of language and words: tests designed to be relatively little affected by differences in verbal ability are said to give a measure of *nonverbal intelligence*.

The score obtained with a properly standardized test may give an indication of the intelligence of a subject which is valuable for many purposes: but it must be remembered that intelligence itself is an abstract concept and as such cannot be measured. What we are actually measuring by these tests is always an individual's *behaviour*, from which the degree of intelligence may or may not be correctly inferred.

8. Intelligence is the rating given to an individual in an intelligence test. This is also described as *psychometric intelligence*.

The intelligence level of an individual is commonly expressed by the *mental age* as determined by an intelligence test standardized for the whole population. The mental age is given by the age of the average child who would obtain the same score as that of the individual tested. The Stanford-Binet test is the test most generally used. *Relative intelligence* may be expressed by the *coefficient of intelligence*, which is obtained by dividing an individual's score by the score that is normal for his age.

The *Intelligence quotient*, or IQ, is the ratio of the mental age of an individual to his chronological age, expressed as a percentage. It gives an index of the mental development (retardation or advancement) of a child, but since it has been shown to be unreliable it is no longer widely used.

LIFE

Common Language
1. Life is the *principle* determining the growth, reproduction and other characteristic activities of plants, animals and all living organisms, and which distinguishes them from inanimate matter.
2. Life is the *period* of practical existence of anything. Thus we can speak of the life of the government, of an institution, of a motor car, or of a living plant or animal. The life of a species may be regarded as a continuum in which an individual being is the temporary expression of an interaction between a particular environment and a specific set of genes. *Human life* is commonly taken as the period from birth to death, but there has been considerable controversy over the essential features of individual life and the precise time when human life begins and ends. The life of an individual can be taken to start with the fertilisation of the ovum at the time of conception, but the developing embryo is at first only a small cluster of cells which lacks the qualities characteristic of a live human being. Thomas Aquinas, the thirteenth-century Dominican, taught that the advent of the human soul occurs at about the fortieth day, but the *conscious* life of a human individual does not start until much later, at about the time of birth. Electrical acitivity in the nervous system is detectable only after about thirty days.

132

Human life can be said to end when the body ceases to function, but different organs of the body may cease to function at different times. Breathing and feeding may continue long after the brain has been damaged and consciousness is lost. The end of human life can reasonably be taken as the time of *brain death*, which is when the brain is damaged to such an extent that consciousness can never be regained.

3. Life is a particular *way of living*, in relation to circumstances, surroundings or behaviour. A person can be said to live a town life, a village life, a saintly life or a life of squalor.

4. Life is the *liveliness*, vigour or animation in an entity such as a piece of writing, a musical composition, a dance, a play or any similar activity, as well as in a living individual.

5. Life is the *conscious experience* of activity, as in learning, exercising skills, pursuing aims, having adventures and satisfying desires. Hence 'zest for life', 'longing for life'. 'Life is in working' (Churchill), 'there is no wealth but life' (Ruskin).

LIGHT

Common Language

In the Common Language, the word 'light' is used loosely in a number of different senses for (1) visible radiation, (2) a source of visible radiation, (3) an illuminated surface, (4) a condition of space in which seeing is possible, (5) daylight, (6) a window or aperture, (7) anything used to produce a flame or light, such as a match and (8) figuratively for mental illumination or enlightenment and (9) any consideration which illuminates or points to a particular view of a subject.

Physics

10. Light is electromagnetic radiation, or radiant energy, in the range of frequencies associated with vision (wavelengths of about $400\,m\mu$–$750\,m\mu$) and also in the ultra violet $(5\,m\mu$–$400\,m\mu)$ and infra-red $(750\,m\mu$–$1\,mm)$ range of frequencies (i.e. the range of frequencies between

X-rays and wireless waves). It may be noted that the meaning of light in physics differs from the meaning (1) in the Common Language, since the word 'light' is used in physics for radiations in the infra-red and ultra-violet which are invisible to the eye.

The internationally accepted unit of luminous intensity or candle-power is the *candela*, which is defined as equivalent to one-sixtieth of the luminous intensity of a black-body radiator of one sq.cm. at the temperature of solidification of platinum ($2.046°K$). The *Hefner* unit, equivalent to 0.9 candela, is the intensity given by a standard Hefner lamp burning amyl acetate. Luminous intensity is measured by the *luminous flux* emitted from a light source per unit solid angle. The luminous flux is the total visible energy emitted by a light source in unit time: the unit of luminous flux is the *lumen*, which is the flux emitted per unit solid angle, or steradian, by a point source of one candela luminous intensity. A uniform point source of one candela luminous intensity emits 4π lumens of luminous flux. *Visibility* is defined as the ratio of luminous flux to the total radiant energy: it is expressed as lumens divided by radiant energy in units per second.

The *intensity of illumination* of a surface illuminated by a point of light soure of P candela luminous intensity at a distance of r metres, for normal incidence, is given by P/r^2 candela metres.

Law

11. The light from the sky falling on the windows of a building. When light has entered the windows of a building for a period of twenty years, in British law the owner has a right to the continued enjoyment of the light, and no one may deprive the windows (known as 'ancient lights') of a substantial part of the light by erecting a building that is too high or too close to them. The test of this right depends on whether the obstruction of the light is sufficient to constitute a nuisance. The word 'substantial' is hard to define precisely and the criteria are different in the country and in the town, but as a working rule it is generally taken that in a town a building may not be erected so high or so close to the 'ancient lights' that the angle of obstruction subtended by the new building exceeds forty-five degrees.

LOVE

Common Language

Love can have a diversity of different meanings, depending on associated attitudes, feelings and the situations in which the word is used. Love can mean: (1) Deep affection, as in a mother's love for her children. (2) An attitude of devotion, as in love of God. (3) Sexual attraction and desire, as in love of a mate. (4) Sexual gratification, as in making love. (5) A strong liking for something agreeable, as in love of sport. (6) An attitude of dutiful commitment, as in love of one's country, and (7) An unfailing readiness to seek another person's good, even at the expense of one's own desires, as in the Christian commandment *'Love Thy Neighbour'*.

Many young people are genuinely puzzled by the meaning of love, and since every one's experience of love is individual, it cannot easily be defined for those who have never experienced it. William Blake distinguished between the immature, possessive child's love:

> 'Love seeketh only self to please,
> To bind another to its delight . . .'

and the unselfish generous love of a mature person:

> 'Love seeketh not itself to please,
> Nor for itself hath any care,
> But for another gives its ease,
> And builds a Heaven in Hell's despair'.

A similar point was made by Overstreet (*The Mature Mind*, 1950): 'Whenever we experience a genuine love we are moved by this transforming experience toward a capacity for goodwill. Or we might put the matter inversely: if what we call in relation to one person or to a few people creates in us no added capacity for goodwill toward many, then we may doubt that we have actually experienced love.'

The love of one person for another, as of a man for a woman, is a state of emotional arousal generally associated with feelings which may include warm affection, sexual attraction, happiness, trust, caring and goodwill. As love develops, the emotional feelings can reach a high level of passionate intensity. It has been said that at that stage 'love is blind'. Later, as love matures, it may become less passionate in nature but associated increasingly with deeper feelings of mutual appreciation, understanding, trust, gratitude and goodwill. With increasing age, the sexual component of love may decrease, the dominant feeling becoming the desire for the happiness and welfare of the one who is loved.

LUCK

Common Language
1. Luck means determination by chance, or according to unknown laws of probability. When a coin is tossed it is a matter of luck whether it will come up 'heads or tails'.
2. Luck can be believed to be the influence of supernatural agents. Superstitious people believe that magic charms can bring them good luck.
3. Luck can mean the operation of factors which are unknown or unforeseen. A misfortune such as an accident or an illness may be regarded as bad luck.

Some apparently irrational ideas about luck can be traced to situations that existed in the past but are now forgotten. Thus the idea that it is unlucky for thirteen people to sit together at a table has survived from times when witch-hunting was rife. A meeting of thirteen (the number of a witches' coven and a devil) was sufficient to arouse the suspicion that they were practising witchcraft, for which the penalty in the ecclesiastical courts was death.

MARRIAGE

Common Language
Marriage is a relationship sanctioned by a community and entered into by two persons of opposite sex who thereby generally agree to live together, to have sexual intercourse, to provide for any children they may have and to help each other as husband and wife. Individual marriage relation-

ships vary widely in character, depending on the religious affiliations of the marriage partners, on the legal commitments involved and on cultural factors operating in the country in which the marriage takes place.

In some countries marriage is still the exception rather than the rule. Thus in the West Indies marriage is widely regarded as a mark of upper middle class status and some seventy per cent of all children are born to unmarried parents. In many countries one marriage does not preclude a second marriage. A Mohammedan may take four wifes, but in other countries this would be regarded as an offence against the law. In parts of Samoa marriage confers on the man sexual rights not only towards his wife, but also towards his wife's younger sisters. The meaning of marriage also varies according to the conditions under which a marriage may be terminated.

In Britain there have been several changes in the marriage relationship. In Roman times it was reported that 'wives are shared between groups of ten or twelve men, especially between brothers and between fathers and sons; but the offspring of these unions are counted as the children of the man with whom a particular woman cohabits first' (Julius Caeser, 54 BC). The Christian churches taught that marriage was indissoluble and should be solemized at a marriage ceremony at which the marriage partners vowed to love and honour each other and to restrict their sexual relations to each other all their lives. They taught that extra-marital intercourse or adultery was a sin. There thus developed two different types of marriage, the one commonly known as 'big marriage' which was performed by the church, and 'little marriage' which could be registered in a Registry Office. The 'little marriage' consisted essentially of a legal contract to give mutual assistance and safeguard the interests of the children. In the Roman Catholic community the right of marriage was restricted by the demand that both partners must be of the same religion, and a relationship not solemnized by the church was described as 'concubinage'. Other types of marriage were also commonly accepted by different sections of the community. As recently as 1792 in the mining villages of Wales many marriages were 'on approval', which meant that if the marriage partners found they did not suit each other, or if the wife was unwilling to move where her husband went to obtain employment in another area,they were free to cancel their marriage contract.

In the Western world an important reason for two people to marry is mutual attraction, and marriage is commonly regarded as a normal culmination of romantic love 'marriage of true minds'. But in some countries many people find their partners through marriage agents or through advertisments in the press, and the resulting marriages are more in the nature of a business deal. In Eastern countries such as India *arranged marriages* are a general custom. The parents commonly arrange the marriage of their children, often at quite an early age, and many young do not even see their brides before the wedding day. Several years may pass before young girl brides are finally led to the husbands' homes, where their union may be established symbolically by tying them loosely together with a rope.

In recent years the situation of married couples has been affected by the development of effective contraceptive procedures and by the increased availability of labour-saving devices in the home, which make it easier for wives to go out to work. This has also been assisted by the provision in some areas of day nurseries which are able to care for the children of working parents. The development of effective contraceptives has also influenced extra-marital relations, which, although still condemned as sinful by the churches, are not contrary to the law and have significantly increased in some countries in certain sections of the community. In many Western countries a proportion of married couples (about one in three) now change their marriage partners by divorce and remarriage, although that it also condemned by the Christian churches.

The word 'marriage' is used both for the marital relationship and for the wedding ceremony or other rite by which the relationship is established. The word is also used in a different sense to desribe a loving relationship of two of the same sex, as 'the marriage of true minds'.

Law
Laws determining the nature of marriage, and therefore

138

affecting the meaning of the word, vary considerably in different countries. Besides differences in the methods of establishing the union (religious, civil, common law) there are differences in matters such as ownership of the wife's property, control of finances, assistance by the wife in the man's work (as in a farmer's, hotelier's or doctor's wife), toleration of extra-marital relationships, the dissolubility of marriage and general conjugal rights. In some countries, but not in the UK, a male member of the Royal family or a titled nobleman can undergo a form of union known as *morganatic marriage*, with a woman of inferior social class. The children of such a marriage are regarded as legitimate, but they are denied the right to inherit their father's rank, titles or possessions. *Child marriage* has been illegal in India since 1928, but the practice is still widespread. According to the *Times of India* there were more than 40,000 child marriages in 1985 in the state of Rajasthan alone. In the *arranged marriages* established in Sikh communities an important factor is the dowry provided by the family of the bride, and there have been many instances of young brides being burnt to death when disputes over the payment of the dowry have arisen.

In many countries mental illness or mental subnormality can be a bar to marriage, and thay can serve as grounds for a petition for annulment or divorce, but in countries such as France, Italy and Spain in which the civil law is influenced by the Roman Catholic church, the mental disorder of a marriage partner is not accepted as grounds for divorce.

There are many countries in which polygamy is accepted as legal and a man has the right to have several wives. There are also some matriarchal communities in which a woman can have several husbands (polyandry). In one of the Berber tribes in the Atlas mountains which resisted Islamic and Arab invaders the queen Kahena had no fewer than 400 husbands. Polyandry is also customary in some tribes in the Belgian Congo.

Since inbreeding can result in children who are mentally or physically handicapped, most countries have laws prohibiting the marriage of brother and sister, father and daughter or others closely related by blood. In the UK under Common Law the prohibition applies also to such

139

persons as stepfathers and step-daughters who are related by marriage and not by blood; but such couples who are related only by affinity can apply for a special Private Marriage (Enabling) Bill which allows them to marry if it is granted by the House of Lords. Most countries permit *mixed marriages* of people of different ethnic groups, but in South Africa the laws forbid the marriage of citizens who are black to those who are white. In the UK marriages are forbidden if they may result in unions which conflict with the immignation laws.

Common Law Marriage is a union in which a couple live together and may have children without being legally married.

MATERIALISM

Materialism has several different meanings. Thus the word has been used for:

> (a) a *philosophical doctrine* developed by the Greek philosophers in discussing the question of whether the universe is better described in physical terms as derived from matter, or in psychological terms, as a construction of the mind,
> (b) a *belief* or *opinion* held in particular by many scientists concerning the existence of supernatural spirits,
> (c) a practical *way of life* based on material values,
> (d) a *socio-economic theory* (historical materialism) put forward by Karl Marx to account for social changes in the community, and
> (e) a *philosophical theory* (dialectrical materialism) developed mainly by Engles as a guiding principle for the Communist Parties.

Like many other words with political or moral implications, materialism has been misrepresented by its opponents. In some of its meanings, materialism is opposed to idealism; but the different meanings of materialism cover so wide a range that it is possible for a person to be a

140

materialist in one sense of the word and an idealist in another. Thus Pavlov, Maudsley, and others were materialists in their denial of the existence of supernatural beings: but in other respects they were high-minded idealists. Various meanings of materialism are indicated in the following definitions:

Philosophy
1. Materialism is the doctrine that all phenomena in the universe, both mental and physical, are ultimately derived from matter and its movements and combinations. Thought, consciousness, will, imagination, conscience and other attributes of 'mind' are all regarded as products of material organisation in a material brain.

Materialism denies the separate existence of mind and matter (*dualism*). In regarding mental and physical phenomena as both ultimately derived from a single primary principle, materialism is a form of *monism*: but materialism is directly opposed to the monistic doctrine that 'mind' or 'spirit' is the primary principle (idealism). Among the Greek philosophers, the Stoics and Epicureans were materialists: more modern materialists include Hobbes, Büchner, Haeckel and many scientists,
2. Materialism is sometimes defined as the view that matter is the only kind of reality: but this is unsatisfactory as a definition unless 'reality' is also defined.
3. Materialism is the belief in the objective existence of matter (Berkeley). The philosophied concepts of materialism have been deserited as *metaphysical materialism*.

Theology
4. Materialism is the disbelief in, or deial of, the existence of supernatural spiritual beings. This implies disbelief in a life hereafter in another world (immortality). It is opposed to the teachings of Christian and other churches.
5. Materialism is the belief that spiritual values cannot be divorced from men and women: that the 'spirit' is not independent of matter. Materialism in this sense of the word accepts the 'reality' of higher spiritual values, but denies that they are in any way supernatural.

Science

6. Materialism is the belief that men and women, like other living organisms, confirm to the laws of Nature; and that the scientific method is applicable at all levels, although physicochemical explanations are inadequate to deal with all phenomena.

7. Materialism is the belief that all things can be explained in scientific terms: that matters of mind and spirit can be reduced to matters of chemistry and physics. This concept of materialism is possibly due to a misunderstanding or misrepresentation of the scientific approach; for scientists do not claim that everything in the universe can be explained in physico-chemical or any other terms.

8. Materialism is the belief that the world investigated by science is the only world of which we need take account: that reality can be identified with that which is measurable or expressible in scientific terms. This implies the refusal to accept any higher values than those expressible in physical terms. This concept of materialism may again be due to misunderstanding of the scientific attitude. Since Galileo (1596–1650), scientists have recognized the existence of values which cannot be measured or expressed in scientific terms.

9. Materialism is a way of life motivated by the pursuit of material comforts rather than idealistic aims.

10. Materialism is an attitude based on the belief that life on earth is our only life; so that we may as well make the best of it. The belief that, instead of preparing ourselves for a life hereafter, we should enjoy life while we can.

11. Materialism is a way of life given up to the sordid pursuit of money and personal advantage, putting material values before spiritual. Materialism is the belief that only sensuous desires are real and worth satisfying: that it is foolish to do anything except for personal gain. This concept of materialism may have arisen from misrepresentation. In this sense of word 'materialists' carries an implication of condemnation, so that it is practically a term of abuse.

Sociology

12. *Historical materialism* is a theory of the determination of

142

historical events by material factors: it was developed by Karl Marx and published in the *Communist Manifesto* (1848). According to this theory, the capitalist system leads to instability and ultimately to revolution, since it creates through the operation of material economic forces a proletarian class which is necessarily opposed to it and bound eventually to overthrow it.

13. *Dialectical materialism* is a philosophical theory of Karl Marx developed mainly by Engles: it recognizes the existence of many different levels of complexity of organization in the world, and it interprets these levels as successive stages in a world-process leading from original chaos to the synthesis of higher forms of organization of increasing complexity. In this context 'dialectical' means 'synthetic'. The gradual development of social organization from states of primitive barbarity to more perfect forms of greater complexity is seen as conforming to the world-process of dialectical materialism,. The synthetic world-process is taken to apply not only to social systems, but also to the evolution of higher levels of human achievement in ethics, science and art.

Dialectical materialism has been regarded as a guiding principle which should enable the Communist Parties to achieve the development of new and still more perfect forms of social organization, leading ultimately to the realization of a classless society. Dialectical materialism is 'materialistic' in that it rejects intervention in human affairs by God or other supernatural agencies and assumes that men possess in their own nature the latent capacity for the synthesis of new qualities of a higher order, and for the development of a higher order of social relationships.

Art
14. Materialism is the tendency in art to lay undue emphasis on the material aspects of Nature.

MEMORY

Common Language
In the Common Language, the word 'memory' is used

loosely for (1) the *faculty* by which facts or past experiences are called to mind; 'notes help the memory'; for (2) the *capacity* for remembrance, e.g. for remembering to carry out duties or other observances at the appropriate time; for (3) an individual item, or the total store, of that which is remembered; 'happy childhood memories'; for (4) a *period* during which events are remembered; 'within living memory'; and for (5) an *act* of commemoration, 'in loving memory of'. In the Common Language the concept of memory is sometimes extended to include the capacity to retain learned skills, as for example reading and writing, or driving a car.

Biology
Memory is regarded as a property of certain living organisms, which helps them to adapt to the condition of their environment. Memory may be defined as (6) the capacity of an organism to behave in a way which is modified by previous experience. In this sense of the word memory, which includes motor skills and is not necessarily at a conscious level, includes the capacity for *conditioning* and for *delayed response*, i.e. responding to an external stimulus when there is a delay between the reception of a stimulus and the permitted response to it.

In the term *genetic memory* the word is used in a figurative sense to describe (7) the total store of information contained in the genetic apparatus (chromosomes, etc.) of the living cell. Such information is not acquired by learning; but during embryonic and later development it enables the organism to recapitulate the characteristics inherited from past generations.

The term *collective memory* has been used for (8) specific patterns of behaviour (mating, nest-building, migration) inherited by all members of a species or of a genetic strain.

The term *plasticity* is used by physiologists for the property of undergoing a permanent functional change in response to a physiological stimulus. Memory is not a physiological term.

Information theory
The term 'memory' is used in a figurative sense for (9) the information storage systems incorporated in computers and other machines to control their behaviour.

Neurology

Brain injuries can lead to the selective loss of certain kinds of memory while other kinds remain relatively unimpaired. On this basis it is possible to distinguish roughly between certain specific types of memory which differ in the retention span: (10) *immediate memory*, is temporary and lasts for no more than a few minutes; this is long enough for example to hold a conversation or to perform a simple mental calculation; (11) *recent memory* refers to events during a period extending from about ten minutes to a few months back, and (12) *long-term memory* includes memories of a more permanent kind extending back to childhood. The term (13) *short-term memory*, which is also used, is ambiguous, since it may refer to immediate memory or recent memory or to both. In any case it is generally desirable to state the retention span.

Loss of memory for events in this period immediately preceding a brain injury is known as *retrograde amnesia*; this may be due in part to impairment of recall, since a part of the memory tends to return in time. Loss of memory for events immediately following a brain injury is known as anterograde or *post-traumatic amnesia*, A sense of familiarity, wrongly attributed to memory, is described as the *déjà vu* phenomenon.

Psychology

Memory has been regarded classically as involving several distinct mechanisms; (a) impression, (b) retention, (c) re-emergence or recall and (d) recognition. Learning requires attention, perception and selection of the matter that is retained. Selection is influenced by motivational (affective) factors, and retention by the process of reviewing learned material and consolidating by rehearsal. It has sometimes been assumed that retention requires a physical alteration in the nervous tissue of the brain; this has been called the 'organic memory,' 'memory trace' or 'engram'. Recall may be effected by the activation of a memory trace: it is influenced by suggestion and by emotive (affective) factors.

As in the Common Language, the word 'memory' is used in several different senses. It is used as (14) a general term for the function of reviving (or reliving) past experiences, for (15) the total store of things that can be remembered and for (16) any particular experience that is called to mind. Several special kinds of memory have been described: (17) *Rote memory* is the capacity for reproducing material (which may be meaningless) in the exact form in which it was presented. (18) *Logical memory* is the capacity for reproducing the essential substance or meaning of learned material without the original form. (19) *Visual memory* is a type of memory in which visual imagery is mainly concerned. (20) *Auditory memory* is the memory for sound. The term 'memory' is normally used in psychology for material consciously learned, but the term (21) *unconscious memory* has been used for function conditioned at an unconscious level and later recalled to consciousness. The same term (22) *unconscious memory* is also used in psychoanalysis for emotionally charged material (affects) and ideas which have been repressed, but which may reach consciousness in disguised forms. Psychologists have described as (23) *short-term memory* the retention of sensory impressions which may persist for no more than a fraction of a second: if this term is used it is necessary to state the retention span.

MENTAL DISORDER

Psychiatry
1. The concept of mental illness has changed very greatly in the last fifty years. Madness or lunacy, as it used to be called, has been associated since biblical times with possession by evil spirits and so surrounded by a cloud of superstitious fear. With the gradual recognition that insanity is a form of illness, the terms 'nervous' and 'mental disease' came into use for the conditions of those who become mentally deranged, while those whose mental abilities are impaired from birth or the earliest years of life (including those of low intelligence) were said to be suffering from mental deficiency or mental defect. But insanity is not strictly speaking a disease, and the term *mental disorder* is now generally regarded as the most appropiate term for mental illness of any kind. Mental

disorder implies a dysfunction of the mind or personality producing an undesirable disturbance of the subjective life of the individual or of his relations with other persons or with society.

The more severe forms of mental disorder, in which the individual is liable to become disorientated and lose contact with the outside world, are now called *psychoses*: these include schizophrenia, depressive psychoses, senile psychoses, toxic psychoses, general paresis and other psychotic conditions. Milder forms of mental disorder, in which the subject remains in touch with reality, are called *neuroses* (or *psychoneuroses*): these include anxiety states, depressive states, obsessional states and hysteria. The term *mental subnormality* or *mental retardation* are coming into use to describe the condition of those who are mentally handicapped or defective from birth. A further class of *psychopathic disorder* is recognized by many psychiatrists: in this category are those who show a marked degree of criminal, aggressive or antisocial behaviour without necessarily being of low intelligence.

Law

2. Mental disorder is of legal significance in view of the requirement of an adequate mental capacity for making a marriage, making a will or making a contract. It is also important in connection with the enactments required for specifying the circumstances in which mentally disordered persons may be compulsorily detained in hospital or placed under guardianship either in their own interests or in the interests of society.

In the United Kingdom the older Lunacy and Mental Treatment Acts (1890–1930) and Mental Deficiency Acts (1913–1938) have been replaced by the Mental Health Act of 1959. This Act gives the following definitions: '*Mental disorder* means mental illness, arrested or incomplete development of mind, psychopathic disorder, and any other disorder or disability of mind.'

'*Severe subnormality* means a state of arrested or incomplete development of mind which includes subnormality of intelligence and is of such a nature or degree that the patient is incapable of living an independent life.'

'*Subnormality* means a state of arrested or incomplete development of mind (not amounting to severe subnormality) which includes subnormality of intelligence and is of a nature or degree which requires or is susceptible to medical treatment or other special care or training of the patient.'

'*Psychopathic disorder* means a persistent disorder of personality (whether or not accompanied by subnormality of intelligence) which results in abnormally aggressive or seriously irresponsible conduct on the part of the patient, and requires or is susceptible to medical treatment.'

(See DISEASE, PSYCHIATRY.)

MIRACLE

Common language
Coming from the Latin *miraculum*, a marvel, the word 'miracle' means literally anything that is wonderful or marvellous. The word is now generally used in a more restricted sense for a wonder attributed to divine intervention, such as the miracles attributed to Christ. In ancient times most people believed in miracles, and miracles were regarded as of almost daily occurence: even Pythagoras and Empedocles were credited by the Greeks with performing miracles, sometimes by natural means and sometimes by magic. Belief in supernatural miracles continued to be widespread during the seventeenth and eighteenth centuries, although, with the growth of scientific knowledge, miracles became less frequent in occurrence and many people no longer believed in them. David Hume (1711–1776) pointed out that the evidence for miracles rests almost entirely on human testimony, which is known to be unreliable; and he collected many instances of reputed miracles which had been faked or imposed by fraud. He concluded that the historical evidence for miracles is inadequate: no testimony is sufficient to establish a miracle, unless the testimony is such that its falsehood would be more miraculous than the fact it endeavours to establish.

Confusion arises from the use of the word 'miracle' in two different senses for

(a) the marvels of Nature, which are capable of explanation on a scientific basis, and

(b) marvels conflicting with the laws of Nature, which are claimed to have been performed with the aid of supernatural powers. Different meanings of the word are indicated in the following definitions:

1. A miracle is a wonderful, extraordinary or lucky occurrence. (e.g. *'It was a miracle that they all survived the accident.' 'Her performance was a miracle of skill'*!)

2. A miracle is a natural event of a particulary impressive kind. (e.g. *'The stars in the heavens are a miracle beyond comprehension'*!)

3. A miracle is an event which is not explainable in scientific terms and which must therefore be attributed to supernatural agencies. (e.g. the miracles said to have been performed by Christ, such as walking on water and raising the dead to life. Miraculous powers have also been ascribed to inanimate objects, such as sacred bones.)

4. A miracle is an illusion of a supernatural occurrence, arising from the misinterpretation of natural events by ignorant and superstitious people, or deliberately created by fraudulent means (e.g. *'One of the principal weapons of anti-religious propaganda in the Soviet Union after the Revolution consisted of demonstrations of how bogus miracles, such as weeping statuettes, could be contrived.'*)

Theology
Miracles have been put forward as proof of the truth of the Christian, Mohammedan and other religious faiths: but since the evidence for miracles rests mainly on historical reports which cannot be verified, it is hard to judge between the conflicting claims that are based on them. Some reported miracles are probably explainable in modern scientific terms: thus the historical accounts of the healing of the sick correspond closely to the removal of hysterical blindness, hysterical paralyses and other hysterical symptoms as is done in modern psychiatric practice. In the present age, instead of promoting belief, the miracles have become an obstacle to belief: churchmen have there-

fore sought to make the miracles of the Gospels more acceptable by interpreting them on a rational basis, or by regarding them as primarily symbolic or mythical in character. 'The old view of miracles as breaches in natural law belongs to a supernatural dualism which modern science has rendered obsolete' (Bishop Barnes).

5. 'A miracle is a happening outside the order of all created nature; therefore God alone can work miracles by His own proper power, since He alone is not a creature.' (Thomas Aquinas).

The definition of a miracle as a breach of natural law due to the intervention of God, has been the subject of considerable controversy. If a natural law can be broken, its validity as a law is questionable. It may also be questioned if it is logical to postulate the existence of an omnipotent power whose capabilities are limited.

6. A miracle is a sign or symbol of the love of God.

7. A miracle is a myth expressing in poetical form the power of God and God's supremacy over all material things.

NEGLIGENCE

Common language

1. Negligence means the lack of care in attending to duties, obligations or proprieties. The word is used for different kinds of behaviour which vary greatly in the degree of associated blame. Thus, it is used for relatively trivial forms of carelessness, such as inattention to the minor details of personal appearance or hygiene: but it is used also for inexcusably callous behaviour showing a complete disregard for the life and safety of others. To the general public, familiar with the phrase 'criminal negligence', the word is commonly taken to imply a high degree of guilt, especially when used in connexion with professional duties or obligations. For this reason professional men are sometimes forced to take extreme action to protect themselves from the finding of 'negligence', which is commonly used in a different sense in law.

Law

2. English law recognises two kinds of negligence, civil and criminal. *Civil negligence* is a civil injury or wrong (tort), for which the remedy is damages determined by the court. Negligence may be defined as the breach of a legal duty to take care, which results in damage, undesired by the defendant, to the plaintiff. Negligence can arise only if there are present together the three elements (a) a legal duty to take care, (b) a breach of that legal duty and (c) damage to the plaintiff arising from the breach. In an action arising from the breach of statutory duty, the damage must be that which the statute was designed to avoid, and not other damage that may have resulted from the breach.

Many claims for negligence are settled out of court, the amount of damages being agreed between the parties privately. If negligence is denied, or the damages cannot be agreed, the case may be taken to court. The burden then rests on the plaintiff to prove (a) that the defendant was negligent and (b) that his negligence caused the damage. In the case of an accident which might have arisen in more than one way, the plaintiff must establish that it was in fact due to the defendant's negligence. Where a case is brought against a professional man, it cannot be taken that he should be infallible, or even that he should use the highest degree of skill; the requirement is only that he should take reasonable care and bring 'a fair, reasonable and competent degree of skill'.

In many cases the negligence lies only in the omission of some relatively minor statutory requirement, which has been followed by a train of events far more serious than the essential error or omission. Thus failure to fill in a form correctly or an excusable delay, owing to the pressure of other duties, in the notification of an Authority, may result in a person being found 'negligent' at law.

3. *Criminal (culpable) negligence* differs from civil negligence in that it shows so little consideration for the life and safety of others that it merits punishment, apart from damages to recompense the sufferer. The degree of negligence must be criminal.

OBESITY

Common Language

1. Obesity means a condition of excessive fatness, stoutness, corpulence or over-weight.

The concept of obesity can hardly be considered without reference to the ethical implications associated with the word. These vary widely in different countries. Thus the significance of obesity in countries where physical fitness is highly prized and abstinence is esteemed as a virtue, is clearly different from that in countries where malnutrition is common and size tends to be equated with vigour and strength.

2. Obesity is commonly defined in statistical terms as the percentage excess of the body weight over an 'ideal' or 'normal' body weight dependent on age, height and sex. Tables of 'normal' body weights are issued by the insurance companies. These generally give mean figures calculated for a population in a particular country, but they ignore individual variations in body-build, which can account for variations of five per cent or more in body weight. Such tables are also unsatisfactory in that they take no account of the economic and cultural differences in different communities. The 'normal' body weights for the USA are higher than those for Great Britain, and mean values vary in different sections of both communities.

3. It is sometimes taken that an excess of ten per cent or more over the 'normal' body weight constitutes 'obesity'. But there is no agreement as to the precise threshold at which obesity begins: some have taken ten per cent, others fifteen or twenty per cent. For this reason estimates of obesity in the population have varied widely and such indices of obesity are unsatisfactory.

Medicine

4. Obesity is the accummulation of an excessive amount of fatty (adipose) tissue. It is recognized that body weight is not a satisfactory index of obesity, since it fails to distinguish between fatness (adiposis) and fleshiness: thus an athlete may be graded as overweight on account of his muscular development, although having less than the

152

normal amount of body fat. A diagnosis of obesity should be based on an individual examination which may be aided by the use of calibrated skinfold calipers; and full consideration should be given to the sex, age, height, body build, occupation, hereditary and other relevant factors.

Many factors may contribute to the causation of obesity. It is usual to distinguish (a) alimentary or exogenous obesity due to overeating from (b) endocrine or endogenous forms of obesity due to metabolic abnormalities. Endogenous forms of obesity include (c) hypogonadal obesity, associated with dysfunction of the sex glands, (d) hypothyroid obesity, due to dysfunction of the thyroid glands and (e) hyperinterrenal obesity due to hyperfucntion of the suprarenal cortex.

5. Obesity may be defined as an excessive proportion of body fat to the total body weight. The normal subject has about ten per cent fat, as measured by radiological, specific gravity or chemical methods. The presence of more than twenty per cent of fat is generally regarded as excessive.

Psychiatry

6. Obesity may occur as a symptom of neurosis, in which the gratification of the appetite for food is substituted for other forms of gratification. On this view, obesity may be conceived as a symptom resulting from anxiety and deprivation.

OBSCENITY

Common Language

1. Obscenity is anything expressed in words, writings, pictures, gestures or in any other medium, which violates established social conventions of fitness, especially in respect to sexual, excretory or other bodily functions.

2. Anything regarded as morally polluted, shocking, offensive to modesty, morally foul. 'Obscenity' is a relative term since it depends on conventions which vary in different societies and in different sections of society at different times.

Law

3. Section 1 of the Obscene Publications Act (1959) states that 'an article shall be deemed to be obscene if its effect or (where the article comprises two or more distinct items) the effect of any one of the items is, if taken as a whole, such as to tend to deprave and corrupt persons who are likely having regard to all relevant circumstances, to read, see or hear the matter contained or embodied in it'.

Section 4 (i) states that 'a person shall not be convicted of an offence and an order for forfeiture shall not be made if it is proved that publication of the article in question is justified as being for the public good on the ground that it is in the interests of science, literature, art or learning'.

Lord Parker ruled 14 April 1964 that obscenity is not confined in law to sexual matters: it includes any material which can corrupt or deprave, as for example in leading to drug addiction.

In November 1971 Lord Widgery ruled that whereas a single publication, such as a novel, should be judged as a whole, in the case of an article with a number of items, such as a magazine or newspaper, the proper test of obscenity is to apply the test of obscenity to each individual item. If one item is found obscene, then the whole article is obscene

Since obscenity varies with the circumstances and the social culture, it is hardly possible to obtain a precise legal definition that will apply under all conditions. The terms 'depravity' and 'corruption' have no clear legal definition; nor is it clear who are those whose minds are open to corruption.

Related terms

Indecency means an act, conduct or behaviour which violates social conventions, especially with regard to sexual relations or dress; as indecent exposure or indecent assault.

Pornography meant originally the depiction of prostitution: by extension it now means the depiction in writing or in pictorial form of material which is sexually stimulating and obscene, especially if exploited for private gain. Pornography has been divided into (a) 'soft porn', which relates to natural sexual functions and (b) 'hard porn', which is the depiction of unnatural sexual perversions (sadism, bestiality, etc) in a way that violently contravenes the current conventions. But it has been said that 'pornography is in the groin of the beholder'; what one person regards as pornographic may not be so regarded by another.

Erotica are writings or pictures relating to sexual arousal, but not specifically obscene.

An unofficial Committee set up by Lord Longford in 1972 proposed wider legal definitions of obscenity and indecency. They would define as obscene anything which 'outraged contemporary standards of decency or humanity which were accepted by the public at large'. They proposed that pornography should be defined by law as that which 'exploits and dehumanizes sex, so that human beings are treated as things and women in particular as sex objects'. These definitions have not been generally accepted at the present time but they are of interest as representing the views of a certain section of the community.

OBSESSION

Common Language
1. The word 'obsession' is used loosely for any persistently held concern, interest, preoccupation or idea: a 'fixed idea'.

Psychiatry
2. An obsession is a thought, impulse, feeling or any other content of consciousness which recurs persistently against a person's wish, with a subjective feeling of compulsion, although it is recognized to be irrational. The main features of compulsion are thus (a) a subjective feeling of compulsion, (b) the wish to resist and (c) the realization that it is irrational.

Obsessions commonly take the form of doubts, compulsive actions, phobias or ruminations, which appear to be isolated from the rest of mental activity. Although recognized to be irrational and actively resisted, the patient is unable to suppress them or prevent their recurring.

PACIFISM

Common Language
The word is of recent origin: it came into use in 1905 and originally referred only to international war. (1) Pacifism is the teaching or belief that international disputes can and should be settled by peaceful means. In recent years the word has often been confused with (2) Christian pacifism, the teaching or belief that violence should never be resorted to as a means of settling a dispute of any kind: if taken to extremes, Christian pacifism can be taken to imply non-resistance, or 'turning the other cheek'. This goes beyond the well-known (Quaker) Peace Testimony of the Society of Friends:

> "We utterly deny all outward wars and strife, and fightings with outward weapons, for any end, or under any pretence whatever; this is our testimony to the whole world."

3. Pacifism, in the sense described by Gandhi and his followers as *satyagraha*, implies non-violent resistance: this may be expressed by active civil disobedience or passive non-cooperation. *Satygraha* is a Sanskrit expression meaning 'insistence on truth'.

PAIN

Common Language
1. Pain is the sensation experienced when the body is injured. It is a feeling characterized by its extreme unpleasantness, and hence by an urgent desire to avoid it. A pain is commonly described in terms of (a) its quality (sharp, dull, aching, throbbing, etc.), (b) location in the body (superficial, deep, etc.), (c) severity, (d) incidence (fleeting, persistent, etc.) and (e) factors that may aggravate or alleviate it.
2. In a wider sense of the word, as a general quality of experience, pain is a concept derived partly from direct personal experience and partly by learning from others and

observing their behaviour. Thus we may judge from their behaviour that other individuals and animals experience pain; but we have no means of knowing if their experience of pain is the same as our own.

3. *Mental pain* is the emotion of sorrow, grief, anguish or distress that may be experienced, for example as a result of failure, loss, or damage to self-esteem. It is the opposite of pleasure. Mental pain differs quantitatively from pain sensation, and it is not localized or referable to any physical stimulus. It can be evoked by a thought or a memory at any time, or by the appreciation of pain or suffering in others.

4. The word 'pain' is used in the plural to mean trouble or effort, in phrases such as 'to take pains' and 'to spare no pains'.

Physiology

5. Pain is a specific sensory experience associated with tissue damage and produced in the conscious subject by the stimulation of particular sets of sensory nerves. It forms part of the biological defence mechanisms of the body, and it is associated especially with the withdrawal reflex. Pain sensation conforms to certain criteria of sensory perception in that (a) it is localized, (b) it is perceived by means of receptor organs, and (c) it can be related to stimuli of which the threshold, intensity and duration can be measured. In mammals the pattern of nervous impulses due to pain stimuli is conducted in nerve fibres running from the periphery to the thalamus by the lateral spinothalamic tracts, and it is relayed from the thalamus to the parietal cortex. Pain has been regarded by some investigators as a *special sensory mode*, with specific pain receptors that are distinct from the receptors for heat, cold and touch: but other investigators have concluded that pain is an effect of *overstimulation* of receptors, for heat, cold, pressure, etc. A current view is that pain sensation depends, not on the intensity alone, but on a particular *patterning* of afferent impulses reaching the central nervous system.

Pain implies a threat to the biological integrity of the organism and hence it is associated with a state of physiological and mental stress. The degree of stress depends on the severity of the pain and other factors; but even moderate pain is sufficient to set up a considerable physiological defence or 'alarm' reaction, with a generalised discharge of the autonomic nervous system. In acute pain the associated muscular tension, sweating, blanching of the skin, dryness of the mouth, palpitations, abdominal discomfort and nausea, form a part of the normal subjective experience of pain; and feelings of fear, anxiety, apprehension or insecurity are commonly present. The alarm response may be regarded as a component of the pain experience, but it is distinct from pain perception and it can be dissociated to some extent from pain perception by drugs which influence the one more than the other. Thus alcohol, which changes the threshold of pain perception by only about forty-five per cent, damps down the stress response to a far greater extent, producing a state of relaxation and freedom from anxiety in spite of the pain. A similar dissociation may also be achieved by the prefrontal leucotomy(lobotomy) operation, in which nerve fibres between the cerebral cortex and hypothalamus are cut.

The threshold intensity of a painful stimulus (the lowest intensity that can be experienced) can be measured with a device such as a radiant heat lamp with which heat of variable intensity can be applied for a standard time to a known area of skin. By using a standard source of radiant heat applied for three seconds to an area of 3.5 sq.cm. of skin on the forearm, Wolff (1947) and his collaborators have worked out a scale of relative pain intensities expressible in terms of '*dol*' units of pain intensity. Various pain responses, such as changes in the circulation and sweat glands (psychogalvanic reflex) can also be measured: but pain itself cannot be measured. Pain itself can be evaluated only by the person experiencing it.

Theology
6. The word is derived from the Latin *poena*, meaning penalty or punishment. In Christian countries the concept of pain is coloured by the old teaching that pain is sent by God as a punishment for one's sins. The idea that pain is divinely ordained is the basis of the opposition of ecclesiastical authorities, for example, to the use of anaesthetics in childbirth.

Law
7. In England, the Cruelty to Animals Act, 1876 relates to experiments, *calculated to cause pain*, on living vertebrate animals (other than man). In this context pain is given a specially wide meaning, since a procedure is defined as calculated to cause pain 'if it is liable to interfere in a material degree, with the animal's health, comfort or integrity'. This includes operations carried out under anaesthesia and feeding experiments involving no pain in the ordinary sense of the word.

PEACE

Common Language
Peace means the absence of a disturbance of some kind. Since the nature of the disturbance needs to be specified, peace is a relative term in which the meaning depends on the context in which the word is used. In ordinary language peace may mean the absence of war, of armed confrontation, of civil violence, of social conflict, or of noise. In terms such as 'peace of mind' it means absence of mental disharmony. While the word is generally used in a negative sense, in some contexts it has a positive connotation in implying a state of orderliness, as opposed to disorder or anarchy: it has this meaning in the title 'Justice of the Peace'. 'Peace' can also have a positive connotation in implying a state of concord or harmony. Peace does not mean inactivity or passivity: nor does it imply the acceptance of injustice. In some contexts peace may be taken to imply a state in which men are free from any infringement of basic human rights and free to direct their energies towards constructive rather than destructive ends.

PERIOD

Common Language
1. Coming from the Greek *peri odos*, meaning 'way round', the word 'period' was used in astronomy for the time in which a planet or satellite makes a complete revolution. It is

now used loosely for any portion, extent, course, duration or interval of time, or of any other continuous process such as a life cycle. Thus we can speak of a period of adolescence, a period of history, or a period of recreation.

2. The days of menstruation in the female.

Language
3. A period is a portion of speech or writing forming a complete sentence.

4. (a) A pause such as is normally made at the end of a sentence. (b) A full-stop, which indicates the pause at the end of a sentence.

Mathematics
5. A period is the interval between two successive equal values of a periodic function (ie a function such as a sine-wave which repeats the same set of values at regular intervals when the variable increases or decreases uniformly.

Physics
6. The time required for one complete cycle or oscillation of any continuous cyclical or periodic process, such as a vibration or simple harmonic motion: the interval of time between the recurrence of equal phases. The period (dimension T) is the reciprocal of the frequency.

7. An interval of time, as in sense (1) of the common language. Thus a *half-life period* is the time required for the value of any function to decrease to one half of the original value. The half-life of a radioactive element is the time in which the quantity present would decrease to half the initial quantity.

Music
8. A period is a complete musical sentence.

Chemistry
9. In reference to the *periodic table*, a period is the interval between two elements of similar chemical and physical properties when the elements are arranged in order of atomic number.

PERSONALITY

Common Language
1. Personality is the distinctive pattern of mental and physical traits which distinguish one individual from another: these include outward appearance, way of speaking, mannerisms, social habits, and general behaviour in interacting with other people. Personality is commonly judged by the impression a person gives of himself: it may be described in terms such as 'strong', 'aggressive', 'virile', 'engaging', 'loving' etc. Hippocrates classified personalities of different types on the basis of their character and temperament. He recognized personalities with temperaments which are *choleric*, or quick-tempered, *sanguine*, or confident and cheerful, *melancholic*, or inclined to be depressed, and *phlegmatic*, or passive and slow.
2. A personality is an *individual* with characteristic qualities or a special role in life, such as a TV personality, a twister or a saint. An indication of personality is given by the language a person uses. Up to the age of six to eight the speech of a young child is largely egocentric, reflecting simple, sensori-motor reactions, after which there is an increasing tendency to exchange thoughts with others. Boasting commonly shows a peak at about the age of ten to twelve and then decreases as a person adjusts to the needs of more intricate relationships and organized activities in a complex society. The personality pattern is still reflected to some extent in a person's language responses, which may show distortions, evasions, inhibitions or regressions of which the individual is unaware.

Significant from a social point of view are personality traits which reflect and influence a person's need for human relationships. Some individuals with personalities of a withdrawn type show little desire for fellowship, while at the other extreme are those who show a consistent eagerness for different kinds of relationships with others.

PHILOSOPHY

1. Philosophy is the systematic pursuit of understanding. The word comes from the Greek *philo sophia* meaning 'lover of wisdom' and in the original sense of the word it included

the study of all branches of knowledge, practical as well as theoretical. In this widest sense, philosophy is the study which takes all knowledge for its province. While striving to avoid illusion and error, it tries to reconcile conflicting viewpoints and aims at achieving a more comprehensive kind of knowledge which gives a unified view of the universe as a whole.

2. The word 'philosophy' is also used in a more restricted sense for a particular system, or the teaching of a particular school. Thus we can speak of the various Greek philosophies (Ionian, Eleatic, Platonic, Aristotelian, Stoic and others) which dealt, for example, with particular aspects of ethics, aesthetics, science, logic, mathematics, theology, language, ontology (the theory of reality) and epistemology (the theory of knowledge).

3. Historically, the mediaeval universities recognized three branches of philosophy in which the degree of Doctor of Philosophy could be conferred:

> (a) *Natural philosophy*, which deals with the phenomena of Nature and everything in the physical universe. This is now known as science.
> (b) *Moral philosophy*, which deals with human behaviour in relation to moral values (ethics).
> (c) *Metaphysical philosophy*, which deals with causation, existance, reality and the ultimate nature of things (metaphysics and theology).

4. Academic philosophy of the present day deals mainly with the kind of questions considered in metaphysical philosophy. While free to utilize the findings of any field of investigation, philosophy is not primarily concerned with the factual knowledge of practical experience, which belongs rather to the realm of science. It is also distinguished from theology which offers explanations that rely on divine revelation and the supernatural. Like science, philosophy appeals to human reason, but it deals with questions of a kind that science cannot answer: it deals, for example, with questions concerning the nature of time, reality, determinacy, purpose, mind, matter, language and meaning. Philosophy may be regarded as the critical

examination and study, not of the actual facts of experience, but of the way in which we sense them, reflect about
them and classify them into different categories. There is
no generally accepted definition of philosophy, since
philosophers differ to some extent in their views on the
nature of philosophy. A current view which has wide
acceptance is that philosophy is a system of reasoning that
gives guidance in our use of words and language as symbols
of meaning, and so helps us to find the appropriate
language for the statements of the sciences and arts.

5. The word 'philosophy' is used also in a different sense
for a system of guiding principles and reasoning, which
support a rational approach to practical problems arising in
the ordinary affairs of life. Pragmatic philosophy of this
kind forms a part of most religious, ethical, and political
systems. In this sense we can speak of a person who faces
difficulties in a calm and philosophical way. In England
and the Commonwealth countries, philosophy in this sense
is generally used in connection with ethical or religious
problems: in the United States the word is often used in a
wider context and it is possible to speak of the philosophy
of a piece of research, or of a commercial enterprise.

PHOBIA

As used in the English language this word has two basically
different meanings, since it may be derived either from the
Greek *phobos*, 'fear' or from *phobia*, meaning 'horror' or
'dislike'.

Common Language

1. 'Phobia' is generally used in the common language to
mean aversion, repulsion or dislike. It is used as a suffix in
many compound terms such as Francophobia (= dislike of
the French), which may be contrasted with Francophilia
(= love of the French). Another example is xenophobia
(= dislike of strangers).

Pathology

2. Phobia is used in sense (1) of the Common Language in

terms such as photophobia (= aversion to light). Hydro-phobia (= aversion the water) is another name for rabies, of which a common symptom is an apparent aversion to fluids, associated with difficulty in swallowing them.

Psychiatry
3. In psychiatry a phobia is a persistent morbid fear which the persons experiencing it know to be unreasonable in that there are no adequate grounds for it, but which they are unable to resist. The essential characteristics of a phobia are its compulsive quality and the subjective experience of internal resistance to it. It is thereby distinguished from feelings of fear or anxiety that may be experienced in other circumstances. Phobias may be associated with particular kinds of objects (such as knives, ropes, dirt, spiders, etc.), with situations (darkness, confined spaces, heights, etc.) or with occurrences (cancer, syphilis, murder, poverty, etc.). It is commonly believed that phobias are related to frighten-ing occurrences experienced in early childhood. Thus a person who as a child was scratched by a cat, may later develop a phobia of cats. But this could not be more than a partial explanation, for many people who have been scratched by cats do not develop phobias.
4. A phobia may be conceived as an emergence in disguised or symbolic form of an unpleasant emotional experience unacceptable to consciousness and therefore forced into the subconscious mind. Thus a phobia of knives may be the symbolic counterpart of an aggressive desire to kill, which is repressed as unacceptable to the conscious mind. Similarly, the common phobias of dirt and infection are often symbolic of sexual impurity and the result of sexual behaviour that would arouse feelings of guilt if admitted to consciousness. In this sense of the word, a phobia is a symbolic representation arising through the operation of a specific psychodynamic process.

PHYSIOLOGY

Common Language
Physiology is the branch of biology concerned with finding

out how living things work. Wheras anatomy deals with structure, physiology deals with the functions of the various parts
of living organisms and the mechanisms by which functions
such as breathing, moving and digestion are performed.
Physiology is divided arbitrarily into a number of broad fields
such as *plant physiology, insect physiology, marine physiology* and
mammalian physiology, which depend on the type of organism
studied. It is also divided into special fields based on the functions studied, as in *developmental physiology, reproductive physiology,*
and *neurophysiology. Human physiology* is important in the study of
medicine, since a knowledge of the normal functions of the
body is required to understand what goes wrong in disease.
Certain aspects of physiology have developed to such an
extent that they demand an extensive knowledge of specialized techniques and they are now accepted as separate
biological disciplines: these include *biochemistry, biophysics,*
molecular biology and *pharmacology.* The physiology of behaviour
forms part of the field of *physiological psychology.*

PIRACY

Common Language
1. The act or practice of robbery on or from the sea or on
navigable inland waters.
2. Infringement of rights confirmed by a copyright or
patent.

Law
3. 'Taking a ship on the High Seas . . . from the possession or
control of those who are lawfully entitled to it and carrying
away the ship itself or any of its goods, tackle, apparel, or
furniture under circumstances which would have amounted to
robbery if the act had been done within the body of an English
county' (J Fitzjames Stephen: *Digest of Criminal Law*).

PLANT

Biology
1. A living organism of the vegetable kingdom. The plants

165

described as lower plants include those of relatively simple structure, such as the bacteria, seaweeds, fungi and moulds. The mosses, ferns and horsetails are intermediate in the morphological scale, while the higher plants include grasses, trees and all flowering plants.

The systematic names of the plants are based mainly on the work of the Swedish botanist Carl von Linné or Linnaeus (1707–1778), who classified all known plants into a system in which every one is given a double Latin name. Thus the common primrose and cowslip are named *primula vulgaris* and *primula veris* respectively, where *primula* is the generic name indicating the kind of plant and the second name indicates the individual species. Minor differences between plants of the same species are described as strains or varieties. Species of similar character are grouped together into *genera*, and similar genera into *families*.

Standard names of garden and agricultural plants are given in the *International Code of Nomenclature for Cultivated Plants* (1958), which is distributed by the Royal Horticultural Society, Vincent Square, London SW1.

Industry
2. The plant includes the equipment, machinery, apparatus, installations and fixtures used in carrying out any industrial process or used for maintenance of any building, mine or other establishment: thus it includes heating plant, lighting plant, ventilation plant, chemical plant and electrical plant. In this sense, the word 'plant' is generally used in the singular.

PRAGMATIC. PRAGMATISM

Common Language
Pragmatic means (1) a practical, business-like attitude with more concern for the outcome than for theoretical principles. This word was formely given several other meanings including (2) interfering in other people's affairs, (3) dogmatic, (4) opinionated, and (5) concering community affairs.

166

Pragmatism is (1) the tendency to be pragmatic, hence dealing with things in a practical, matter-of-fact way.

Philosophy
Pragmatism is (2) the doctrine that the meaning of any concept depends in part on its practical consequences in ordinary life. It rejects the idea that truth is absolute, objective and independent of ourselves. William James maintained that we regard as 'true' that which works in practice: 'We cannot reject any hypothesis if consequences useful to life flow from it.' John Dewey held that in forming our opinions most of us are influenced not by reason alone, but also consciously or subconsciously by our personal interests and emotions: truth depends on a process of enquiry which is not entirely objective. Peirce maintained that the meaning of a word or an idea is influenced by the effects of a practical kind which it may have: 'Truth is the opinion which is fated to be ultimately agreed by all who investigate.' The philosophy of pragmatism has been largely rejected by Bertrand Russell and some other philosophers.

History
Pragmatism is (3) a method of studying history in which events are considered with respect to their underlying causes, consequences and lessons which can be learned from them.

Pragmatic means (6) relating to the causes, effects and lessons to be learned from historical events.

PREVALENCE

Medical Statistics
Prevalence is expressed as the number of occurrences in a unit population; as for example the number of cases of sickness per 100,000 at risk, or the morbidity rate. In evaluating prevalence data it is necessary to distiguish between (a) *point-prevalenc*, which is the number of cases per unit population at a given point in time, (b) *period-prevalence*, which is the number of cases per unit population occurring

over a given period such as a month or a year (e.g. the annual referral rate) and (c) *life-prevalence*, which is the number of persons per unit population affected during their lifetime (e.g. the morbidity risk). The *cumulative prevalence* is the total number of cases recorded per unit population from the beginning of a series to the time when the last observation is recorded.

The reliability of prevalence data depends on (a) the precision with which the observed occurrence is defined, (b) the reliability of diagnosis, (c) the probability of cases presenting for examination, (d) the probability of identified cases being reported and (e) the absence of religious or other bias which can lead to misrepresentation or falsification of reports. For comparative purposes differences in average age, in sex and in mean life expectancy of the populations must generally be taken into account.

See FREQUENCY

PROVOCATION

Common Language
1. Derived from the Latin *pro-vocare* 'to call forth, to challenge, to excite', provocation is generally used in an unfavourable sense for an act which causes annoyance, anger, resentment or retaliation. In the Common Language the word is used loosely for a provocation act, for (2) the quality of provocative behaviour and sometimes (3) for the state of being provoked. Provocation is a concept which depends on the judgement of a third person, and it is therefore hard to define.

Law
4. Provocation may be pleaded as a defence in a trial for a crime of violence. The defence of provocation may arise where a person's intention to kill or inflict bodily harm 'arises from sudden passion involving loss of self-control by reason of provocation'. Evidence of a provocative incident and nothing more is not enough to establish provocation in law. Provocation in law consists of three elements: (a) the act of provocation, (b) the loss of self-control, both

actual and reasonable, and (c) the retaliation proportionate to the provocation. A credible narrative of events must be produced, which indicates the presence of these three elements; and their relationship to each other, particularly in time, is of the first importance.

5. In International Law, provocation is an act which might reasonably be expected to evoke retaliatory measures.

PSYCHIATRY

Common Language
1. Psychiatry is the medical speciality which deals with the diagnosis, treatment and prevention of mental disorders of every kind and with the care of patients who are mentally disturbed.

Medicine
2. Psychiatry, which is the branch of medicine dealing with the mentally ill, was first practised as an outgrowth of neurology, but it was then strongly influenced by the teachings of Freud, Alder, Jung and others who developed the theories of psychoanalysis. Many psychiatrists then came to use the methods of *dynamic psychotherapy* developed by the psychoanalysts for the treatment of mental patients. While this was helpful to those suffering from the milder types of personality disorders, it was less effective for the treatment of mental illnesses of a more serious kind. The 'drug revolution' of the 1950s then saw the introduction of powerful new drugs which were effective for treating the symptoms of depressive illness, schizophrenia and other disabling mental illnesses, so that many mental patients previously confined to hospital were able to come out and live in the community. The development of *behavioural psychotherapy* introduced another effective form of treatment as an alternative to dynamic psychotherapy. With the application in recent years of new research techniques for studying the biochemical and physiological correlates of normal and pathological human behaviour there then developed the new discipline of *biological psychiatry*. Psychiatric teaching was divided for a time between the views of

the analytical psychiatrists and the more organic views of those who used mainly the methods of biological psychiatry, but at the present time there are many psychiatrists who hold that these two approaches are not incompatible with each other and that psychiatric practice can benefit from them both.

Law

3. The speciality known as *forensic psychiatry* deals with matters such as assessing the mental state of prisoners at the time when they committed crimes and advising the courts on the treatment they should receive. The recognition of forms of mental abnormality which can result in diminished responsibility can reduce the charge and the punishment given to a prisoner for an offence.

Traditionally the psychiatrist, like the physician, was hired to act as the patient's agent and to put the patient's interest first in helping them to overcome their mental illness and relieve their discomfort. It may be noted that in some countries psychiatrists are now expected to act rather on behalf of the state hospitals, prisons, courts and military or prosecuting authorities, which employ them, and not as the patient's agent. This change in the traditional relationship, which gives a different meaning to the word 'psychiatrist' and therefore to the practice of psychiatry, has been criticised in other countries as liable to lead to misunderstanding and abuse.

RATIONAL. RATIONALISM

Common Language

Rational means (1) reasonable, sensible and sane, or acceptable to people of good judgment. The word 'rational' is also used in a narrower sense to describe (2) views established by sound reasoning, as distinct from those based on authoritative statements, divine revelation or dogmatic assertions of any kind.

Philosophy

Rationalism is a principle which stresses the importance of

170

reasoning, rather than feelings or individual observations, as the main basis of truth, knowledge and understanding. It is opposed to the sensationalist or empiric reliance on the senses or on practical experience as the primary sources of knowledge.

Theology
Rationalism is a doctrine which regards reason as the chief or only reliable guide to truth in matters of religious doctrine. It does not accept divine revelation and it seeks to explain in a rational way events which are regarded by some as supernatural.

It can be confusing that the word *'rationalisation'*, and the verb 'to rationalise', which originally meant explaining on a rational basis, have come to have a second meaning in the sense of explaining away even by false reasoning, and thereby trying to discount the significance of reports of miracles and other events under consideration.

REALISM

Common Language
1. Realism is a way of thinking that attaches greater importance to a knowledge of real facts than to what is theoretical or imaginary in dealing with human problems. Realism is a rational, down-to-earth attitude that rejects vague idealistic pretensions and wishful thinking: it aims at a practical solution of problems based on a true under-standing of the realities of life.

Art
2. Realism is a name that has been given to certain movements and traditions in literature and the graphic arts, which emphasize the value of portraying subjects that exist in real life. Realism is associated particularly with a group of nineteenth-century painters (Courbet, Millet, Manet), who rebelled against the artificiality of the romantic and neo-classical traditions: instead of painting mythological, biblical or romantic inventions, they turned for their subject matter to everyday contemporary life. Others who

have contributed notably to realism in the arts are the painters Constable, Corot, Daumier and Leibl. Associated with realism in this sense of the word is the teaching that the beauty of a work of art derives from its correspondence with Nature.

3. Realism is the accurate detailed representation in literature or art of real scenes, often of a sordid, ugly, or unpleasant kind. Examples of such realism are Goya's etchings depicting the horrors of the French invasion of Spain and Rousseau's *Confessions*, in which he described his relations with a servant girl.

Philosophy

4. The term 'realism' has been applied to a number of philosophical doctrines which hold that the objective physical world has an existence independent of the mind's perception of it. This is the opposite of idealism (which holds that mind and ideas alone exist).

5. Realism is the teaching of the medieval scholastics (Thomas Aquinas) that general ideas or universals are the only things that have a real objective existence; all other things are merely names or ideas.

6. Realism is the view that it is possible to have knowledge of the objective world by direct intuitive awareness or observation of objects and events.

Education

7. Realism is the view that knowledge must be of the realities of life, not of verbal formulae or abstractions. On this view it is argued that students should be taught about the contemporary, concrete world rather than metaphysical or classical subjects.

REALITY

Common Language

1. Reality is the factual or underlying truth as distinguished from outward appearances. In this sense of the word the realities of the external world may be regarded as imposing conditions on our behaviour to which the individual must adapt.

2. Reality is the impression of the world we live in arising from direct observation of objects and events: perceptual reality. This view of reality, commonly held by children, ignores the subjective nature of perception and accepts one's own personal view as a correct picture of how things truly are (Piaget). It is the view of reality of those who accept as real whatever they themselves feel and perceive.

3. Reality is a subjective private concept of objects and events in the external world. In this sense reality is accepted as being a personal concept different for each one of us, depending on age, individual perceptual mechanisms, language and cultural background. Thus the reality of a butterfly may be different for a child, for an artist and for an entomologist. Reality depends also on our mental state at any particular time: thus our idea of reality may be distorted by anxiety, depression, euphoria or desire.

4. Reality is the totality of material objects and events directly measurable in units of length, mass and time: physical reality. This view of reality does not preclude the acceptance of relativity and the identity of energy and mass.

5. Reality is that which is accepted as real, and not imaginary, by most members of a particular community. In this sense of the word a sane man is regarded as being in contact with reality: but the reality of one community is not the same as that of another. Thus in Europe a cow may be regarded as a source of meat; but the Hindu child must accept the reality of a cow as a sacred animal.

6. 'Objective reality' is the concept of reality free from all subjective bias. Since all human views of reality are subjective, a truly objective view of reality is unattainable and objective reality must remain a metaphysical speculation.

REHABILITATION

Common Language
Rehabilitation is the act or process of restoration to a satisfactory physical, mental, vocational or social status after an illness, injury or loss of any kind. The nature of rehabilitation depends on the goal, which may be restora-

tion to good health, restoration to a former position, or re-establishment of a person's good name. Rehabilitation after illness or injury can proceed in association with therapy. It may involve adjusting to the limitations imposed by disabilities, and the final status may not be the same as that preceding the disorder.

After mental illness the primary goal of rehabilitation is the restoration of social skills, confidence, self-respect and dignity, so that a person can feel loved and wanted, and not rejected by the community. Rehabilitation can be aided by work of an appropiate kind, by contact with caring friends and by activities which help to improve the quality of life in the community.

RELIGION

Common Language

A religion is commonly understood to be a set of teachings and beliefs that strongly influence people's behaviour, their morality and the way in which they lead their lives, but there are many religions which differ widely in the beliefs they uphold, and the meaning of the word therefore varies in different parts of the world. Several religions claim the existence of a supernatural God or gods who are held to have created the world, and who are believed to make personal contact with those who live on earth, giving them the prospect of life after death and other rewards. On that basis it is regarded as a duty for all to worship and obey the God or gods on whom their destinies are held to depend.

The beliefs of the different religions are laid down in the scriptures maintained and taught by groups of clergy in the Churches which operate in many regions. While the behaviour advocated by the Churches is for the most part of an upright, moral, honourable and loving kind, fostering reverence and devotion, they have sometimes become involved in politics to an extent that has been criticised. The influence of a religion on a people's behaviour is not without political significance and a number of investigators have concluded that in the past the primitive religious beliefs of the masses were promoted to a large extent by their rulers as an instrument for their control: 'Religion is the sign of the oppressed creature, the kindliness of a heartless world, the soul of soul-less circumstance. Religion is the opiate of the people' (Karl Marx). Competition between rival religious sects has also led at times to their perpetrating acts of serious cruelty, as happened in former times in the Christian Church when it fostered the Crusades and the Inquisition. At the present time there are still Moslem sects in which it is regarded as a virtue to support a Holy War to exterminate 'infidels' belonging to other religious creeds. Their treatment of wrongdoers by amputating limbs or stoning them to death is also contrary to the teachings of other religious faiths.

Besides the Christians and Mohammedans, those belonging to other religions include the Buddhists, Hindus, Confucianists, Taoists, Shintoists and Jews. There are also many other smaller religious sects. In some religions the Churches continue to uphold fundamentalist teachings, such as the Roman Catholic doctrines of Creation by God, the Virgin Birth, the Resurrection, and the Miracles: but the Buddhists and some groups such as the Humanists do not support belief in the supernatural or insist on the existence of God.

While religion is still regarded by some people as divinely created, there has been a progressive change in people's attitudes and it is now widely accepted that religions are sets of teachings developed by man with the main object of improving behaviour, relieving anxieties giving a sense of dignity, fostering self-esteem and comforting the bereaved. Most religions still rely to a large extent on belief in magic and superstition, and they have little use for logic or reason, but the religious beliefs upheld by the Churches have undergone numerous changes in the course of time and they are gradually being brought more into harmony with modern knowledge. There are now many who accept the views of scientists and are ready to adopt more rational and liberal views.

See GOD, HUMANISM.

REMUNERATION

Common Language
A *wage* or *pay* is a fixed sum of money paid periodically, generally as a daily or weekly payment to a manual labourer or servant in return for the work done. A *salary* is a regular payment made periodically, generally to a non-manual employee on the basis of an annual contract. A *fee* is a sum charged by a professional person such as a doctor or solicitor for a specific service: an *honorarium* is the sum a professional person may be offered or paid for his services rendered. A *stipend* is a fixed periodic payment made generally to a professional person or an official to cover living expenses or other costs incurred in fulfilling an engagement: a stipend may be untaxed. An *allowance* is a sum given without obligation, as for example the pocket-money allowed by a parent to a child. An untaxed allowance may be given to cover expenses incurred in performing duties of any kind. *Remuneration* is any sum of money or other reward received for work done or for services performed.

SANCTION

Common Language
1. The authorization, permission or consent given by a superior authority for an action of their subordinates or of others who require such permission.

Law
2. A penalty imposed for breaking a law or for inducing its enforcement.

Ethics
3. The justification given for a rule of conduct or for specific behaviour (e.g. *religious or moral sanctions*).

SCIENCE

Common Language
The word is commonly used for (1) the study of the facts of

nature, or natural science as a whole, and also for (2) recognized branches of experimental science such as chemistry, physics and biology as well as psychology and sociology. *Pure science* of this kind is generally distinguished from *applied science*, or technology, which is the application of science in agriculture, industry, medicine and other practical fields.

Philosophy

'Science' is a word which has changed considerably in meaning since it was first introduced. Science originally meant (3) the whole of organized learning and knowledge, including the study of history, philosophy, literature and the arts. The laws of science were regarded by the early scholars as final, unalterable truths. With the gradual development of *experimental science* a distinction arose between the kinds of knowledge gained from subjective experience or by divine revelation and knowledge obtained objectively by experiment. Science then came to be understood as (4) ordered knowledge obtained by systematic observation, experiment and abstraction. Scientific knowledge of this sort was built up through research which involved the collection of data and the formulation of theories and hypotheses which then could be tested by experiment. This led to the establishment of a body of empirical facts and the natural laws of science, and to the development of special fields of investigation such as physics, chemistry and biology, which dealt mainly with different areas of data, but which overlapped to some extent and which are all part of the general field of science.

It has been said that the scientist is a person who knows how to ask questions and carry out invetigations to find the answers (Bernal). The science so developed depends, not only on the facts of nature, but also on the imagination and creative ability of the scientists who invent the hypotheses that can be tested and who devise appropiate experiments for testing them. Thus science begins in wonder and may involve flights of imagination in those engaged in research. An important characteristic of the scientific approach is the 'open mind' or the willingness of the scientist to reconsider any facts or conclusions in the light of new evidence. The laws of science are not retarded as infallible. In this respect science differs from the inflexible dogmatic assertions of fact made in some other fields of learning, which claim to be based on final unalterable truths. Thus science replaces the concept of inevitable effect by that of probable trend (Bronowski).

While scientific learning covers a wide area, it must be recognized that it does not include the important range of human experience involved in aesthetic, compassionate, inter-personal, visionary and other kinds of human feeling, which cannot easily be measured or defined. It cannot therefore be said that science provides a complete picture of the nature of things. The reductionist view that science is the only valid form of knowledge and that everything can ultimately be explained in terms of the behaviour of elementary components is therefore not a part of modern science. While the meaning of the word 'science' in the English language is now limited to experimental science, that distinction is not made in some other languages such as French and German. Thus the German word *Wissenschaft* includes not only natural science, but also the systematic study of history, philology and philosophy as well. This can cause difficulties in the translation of texts from other languages into English.

SENSE. SENSATION

Common Language
The word *sense* has several different meanings.
1. The five senses of the body, sight, hearing, taste, smell and touch are faculties of perception mediated by *sense organs* (nerve structures), which receive signals bringing information from the external world or from within the body and transmit them to the brain. The term *sixth sense* is used for a postulated inner faculty of intuition, which may present information that is correct, but which is not of the same validity as the information received through the five recognized senses of the body. The adjective *sensory* means connected with or related to a sense, a sense organ, sense data or a bodily sensation.

178

A *sensation* is (a) the feeling consciously experienced when a sense organ is excited (colours, sound, smells, tastes, warmth, cold, etc.). A sensation can also mean (b) a more general bodily feeling such as fatigue, anger, anxiety or grief. A further meaning of sensation is (c) a state of emotional excitement which may be aroused in an individual or a community by an unexpected or sudden event such as assassination, a political upheaval, a new artistic creation or a scientific discovery. The adjective *sensational* is applicable to anything likely to arouse a strong emotional reaction or provoke excitement, such as a political development, a striking work of art, an actor, a musician, or a scientific discovery.

Sensuous means related to enjoyable sensory experience or luxurious indulgence.

Sensual, which can have a derogatory implication, means related to sexual gratification, carnal, lustful or lewd.

2. In expressions such as 'a sense of pleasure' or 'a sense of wrong' the word *sense* means a type of feeling, perception or recognition induced by a particular situation. In expressions such as 'a sense of humour' or 'a sense of duty' a quality of intellectual perception is implied. The adjective *sensitive* means strongly influenced by sensory stimuli or strongly affected by influences which may be perceived and felt. Hence the word *sensitivity,* which is the capacity to respond to sensory stimulation, or the magnitude of the reaction to stimuli of any kind. We can speak of the sensitivity, not only of living creatures, but also of plants and inanimate objects such as measuring instruments etc. *Sensibility* is the capacity to experience through the senses (it does not mean 'being sensible').

3. When a word or expression can have different meanings, the *sense* in which it is used is the meaning given to it in any specific context. The sense of a communication is the particular interpretation or significance given to it, or the meaning it is intended to convey.

4. In expressions as 'to talk sense' or 'it makes good sense' the word *sense* means an attitude or viewpoint based on good sound judgment of a kind that any reasonable person can appreciate. The adjective *sensible,* which is related to this meaning of the word sense means shrewd,

179

wise, practical and of good judgment, or showing good sense. *Common sense* is the ability to see and judge things in a reasonable, practical and sensible way, not relying on extremist doctrines or elaborate hypotheses, but in keeping with the down to earth views of ordinary sane members of the community.

Religion

Belief in the existence of a God has been based by some people on the possession of an *inner sense*, which is an inborn consciousness that God exists.

SHOCK

Common Language

This word is used in a number of different senses to describe a sudden more or less violent event which interrupts the normal state of stability of a system. Thus a physical shock can result from a sudden violent blow or collision. An earthquake shock implies a sudden shake of the earth's surface. A military shock is produced by a sudden charge or violent attack (hence *shock troops*). An electric shock is produced by the sudden passage through the body of an electric current. Mental shock can result from a severely upsetting experience, such as a sudden loss or bereavement, or a violent disturbance in human affairs.

Medicine

Shock is a state of prostration or collapse which occurs in conditions in which there is extensive tissue damage, such as serious wound injuries, burns, infections or acute abdominal disease. Shock is characterized by (1) low blood pressure, (2) rapid, feeble pulse, (3) general muscular weakness, affecting muscles of the limbs, of respiration, of the arteries and of the heart, (4) dilated pupils and (5) pale cold clammy skin. It used to be believed that shock is always associated with a reduction in cardiac ouptut, but it is now recognized that that is not so. Shock may be defined as a syndrome characterized by an acute reduction in the nutritional blood supply to vital tissues, associated with an impaired supply of oxygen and substrates, and inadequate elimination of acid metabolites from the tissues (drainage function).

The causes of shock may be divided into those of sudden and those of more gradual onset. The following different types of shock are recognized. (1) *Haemorrhagic shock* involving blood loss with minor tissue damage. (2) *Traumatic shock* with blood loss, together with extensive tissue injury. (3) *Burn shock* in which there may also be loss of blood plasma. (4) *Dehydration shock* with loss of water and electrolytes. (5) *Cardiogenic shock* in which there may be myocardial infarction with heart tamponade and pulmonary embolism. (6) *Septic shock*, which is associated with severe infection. (7) *Anaphylactic shock* which is caused by an antigen-antibody reaction. (8) *Refractory shock* which denotes a state of shock which does not respond to treatment by the methods available. In animal experiments this is known as *irreversible shock*.

Psychiatry
Shock therapy is a method of treatment of patients suffering from depression or other forms of mental illness. The shock is administered by the use of drugs or by the brief passage of an electric current through a part of the brain. This may cause a temporary loss of memory, but the treatment is generally effective in relieving the mental symptoms.

SOVEREIGNTY

Common language
1. Sovereignty is the authority held by a ruling monarch, or by a parliament or other supreme ruling body.
2. National sovereignty is a collective term applied to the rights, privileges, duties and responsibilities invested in a ruling monarch or, when effective rule has been taken over by a Government, assumed by the state. National sovereignty includes the right of self-government and the right to determine laws and economic regulations: it includes also the right of diplomatic representation in the

community of nations of the World. National sovereignty does not mean the right to do exactly as one may please within the national territory; for it is subject to the duties of honouring treaties and agreements, of respecting international rights of way and of conforming to the rulings of the International Court of Justice. It also carries the responsibility of protecting the lives and property of citizens of other nations. The concept of National sovereignty thus includes the relations of a State (a) towards its own citizens and (b) towards other States.

3. 'Absolute sovereignty' is a doctrine which asserts the right of a State to absolute and unconditional authority, being responsible only to itself. The concept of absolute sovereignty is inconsistent with the requirements of international law, and no State has ever in fact possessed such a right: but the doctrine still persists as an argument of militant nationalism.

Law
4. The word 'sovereignty' is used in a restricted sense for the status of the highest legal authority in a country, e.g. the sovereignty of the Queen in Parliament.

SPIRITUALISM

Common Language
1. Belief in the existence of supernatural spiritual beings, such as ghosts.
2. The teaching or belief that spirits of persons who have died can communicate with the living, either directly or through a 'medium' who has a special faculty for communicating with spirits of the departed. Claims to communicate with spirits have been made from time to time by individuals in many primitive societies, but the use of the word 'spiritualism' in this sense is of relatively recent origin: it dates in fact from the claims made in 1848 by two young daughters of a farmer named Fox in a rural district of America that they could communicate with the dead by raps on a table. Later they made a public confession that their claims were fraudulent and they showed how they

produced the 'raps' by cracking their finger joints. But in the meantime the credulity of the general population was exploited by a number of others who claimed to have similar special powers as 'mediums' and who made money by organizing seances for table-tapping, automatic writing and other supposed means of communicating with spirits of the dead. The mediums were repeatedly exposed as fraudulent, but there remained always some who believed in their claims.

STRESS

Common Language

1. The word 'stress', probably derived from 'distress', was used orignally for any kind of hardship, burden, pressure or compulsion inflicted on a person or on a material object. A stress produces characteristically a condition of tension or strain in the person or object affected by it. The word is now used loosely in several different senses for (2) pressure or emphasis (as in the phrase *to lay stress on*) and particularly for (3) an *adverse force*, pressure or influence. The word is also used for (4) the *state* or *condition* of a person subjected to adverse influences causing tension or strain, and for (5) a *state of affairs* or general situation characterized by adverse influences.

By 'the stress of modern living' is generally understood the sum total of irksome obligations, duties, and social conventions, together with any other conditions of living that may give rise to worry, tensions, anxiety, conflict or frustration. Mental stress may also arise for specific reasons, as in an individual who holds beliefs that are in conflict with the views of those in authority.

Physics

6. Stress is a physical pressure applied to a body so as to cause a deformation of the body: the deformation is called strain. Stress is measured by the force applied per unit area, or dynes per. sq. cm. in cgs units. The dimensions of stress are $M\ L^{-1}\ T^{-2}$. The strain is expressed as the ratio of the change of length to the original dl/l along any axis: the

dimensions of strain are unity. The ratio of stress to strain is a characteristic constant of a body: it is known as the modulus of elasticity.

Biology
7. Stress may be defined as anything constituting a threat, real or apparent, to the biological integrity of the organism. Stress depends partly on factors in the environment and partly on the vulnerability of the individual. There are environmental factors that constitute a stress for one individual and may not be stressful for another who is less sensitive or better able to adapt.

Physiology
8. An environmental agent or influence, affecting an organism adversely (Hoagland, 1955). The word 'stress' is used here in sense (3) of the Common Language, for agents such as heat, cold, etc. (the term *stressor agent* or *stressor* is now commonly used by physiologists for a stress in this sense of the word.)

9. Stress has been defined as the *state* or *condition* of an organism subjected to a load of such strength as to cause a depletion of reserves greater than can be restored in the time available for recovery. In other words, stress is the state of an organism subjected to pressures to which its homeostatic mechanisms cannot readily enable it to adapt.

10. The word 'stress' is also used by some physiologists to describe the *disturbance* or *strain* produced in an organism subjected to a load (Gerard, 1957). In this sense of the word, a stress can be described in terms of the displacement of factors such as blood pressure, blood metabolite levels, etc. which are controlled by the homeostatic mechanisms.

Psychology
11. Stress is the state or condition of an organism whose reaction to the environment is characterized by anxiety, tension, or a defensive behavioural response. Under these conditions people build up defence mechanisms to reduce their anxiety or to defend themselves against it.

Stress itself is an abstract concept derived partly from subjective experience and partly from the observation of overt stress responses in situations that elicit them. The concept of stress may be coloured by views held about the situations that occasion stress and about the psychological mechanisms involved in reacting to it.

Psychological stress situations are generally characterized by a conflict of incentives or of basic drives to which the individual is compelled to adapt. There may be an apparent threat to self-esteem or to security, as when achievement falls short of expectations. Mental stress may be chronic, as for example in unhappy human relationships and long-standing conflicts over religious, political or racial beliefs: or stress may be acute, as in the stress of a cross-examination or the sudden loss of a lover or of a child.

Stress may be produced in an individual experimentally by methods such as giving an insoluble problem to solve. A comparable stress situation can be obtained in animal conditioning experiments in which an animal is made to attempt a discrimination that is too difficult for it. Prolonged stress of this kind can lead to the development of complex defense reactions described as 'experimental neuroses'. The reaction to psychological stress depends in general on constitutional factors making up the personality and particularly on the capacity to adapt by modifying the established pattern of behavioural response.

Stress may be consciously experienced as such, or it may be unconscious and recognized only by the after-effects. Thus individuals may push themselves beyond the limits of endurance without being consciously aware of the stress and thereby impose on themselves a burden from which it may take them some time to recover. The extent to which stress is consciously experienced varies greatly from one individual to another, depending on personality traits as well as on the nature of the stress situation involved.

STRUCTURE

Common Language
1. The arrangement, pattern or grouping of component parts which make up a whole: the way in which a building, an animal body, a sentence, an organisation etc. is put together.

185

Psychology

2. Mental structure is the organized pattern of components which constitute the personality of an individual, and which account for certain types of behaviour under different conditions. Hence *structural psychology* (also known as *structuralism,* or *content psychology*) which deals with the systematic investigation by introspection and experiment of different mental states and experiences, and their analysis into basic elementary constituents. The *structuralist* hypothesis of an underlying structure which can be revealed by detailed investigation and analysis has been helpful in adding to our understanding and clarifying the nature, not only of human consciousness and personality, but also of complex situations of many kinds. *Genetic structuralism* deals mainly with structures of a more basic kind which have developed or changed at different stages of history. The term *structural* implies a certain degree of stability, in contrast to that which is functional or dynamic.

SUICIDE

Common Language

Suicide is the act of intentionally terminating one's own life, of killing oneself.

Law

'Suicide is an act of intentional self-destruction by a person knowing the probable consequences of what he is doing. Self-destruction during a fit of delirium would be misadventure, but not suicide, since suicide requires an intention by the person concerned to kill himself' (Lord Justice Sellers, 30 January 1967).

The Suicide Act (1961) removed suicide from the Criminal Code and recognized it as a medical or social problem. It is recommended by the Ministry of Health that anyone who has attempted suicide should be seen by a psychiatrist.

Psychiatry

Suicide can be a manifestation of any one of a number of

186

different conditions. It is estimated that about a third of those who kill themselves are suffering at the time from a form of depressive illness. In other cases suicide is the reaction of a vulnerable personality to social disorganization, economic hardship or stressful inter-personal relations. Durkheim described a form of 'altruistic suicide' in those such as the aged Eskimo who wishes to avoid becoming a burden on his family.

It is found that for every one person who commits suicide there are six to ten who make an unsuccessful suicidal attempt. Attempted suicide or parasuicide may be undertaken as a kind of gamble with life, when survival is accepted as an act of providence. In many cases attempted suicide represents a 'cry for help' in a person who has reached the limit of endurance. In those who attempt suicide the motivation generally differs from that of those who actually kill themselves. Most people who commit suicidal acts are muddled in their intentions: they have no clear determination to end life, but act rather in the spirit 'I don't care whether I live or die'.

TECHNOLOGY

Common Language
The organized body of facts and principles involved in the application of a set of practical techniques. Thus one can speak of the technology of printing, music, teaching, engineering, medicine or the industrial arts. A technology may be developed by the application of science; but *technology* is not synonymous with applied science.

A *technologist* is a person proficient in a technology. A *technician* is a person skilled in applying a set of techniques. 'Technicians and other supporting technical staff occupy a position between that of the qualified scientists, engineer or technologist on the one hand, and the skilled foreman or craftsman or operative on the other.' (*Triennial Scientific Manpower Survey*, 1965)

See SCIENCE.

THEOLOGY

Common Language
1. The study of the nature and characteristics of a God, or Gods, and their relation to mankind; divinity.
2. The systematic study of the basis and sources of religious beliefs; study of the scriptures, divine revelation, evidence for miracles and related subjects.

Theologians have distinguished *natural theology*, which is based on the interpretation of natural phenomena, from *dogmatic theology*, based on the authoritative interpretation of scriptures by a church. *Pastoral theology* deals with the religious needs of people living in the community. *Clinical theology* is a name given to a form of psychotherapy which attempts to combine Christian theology with the principles of psychoanalysis. It aims at easing the stress and mental pain in individuals with troubled minds by giving them a sense of well-being and a consciousness of status. *Revealed theology* deals with the doctines of faiths such as Christianity or Mohammedanism, which are claimed to have been divinely revealed.

TRIBUNAL

Common Language
1. A tribunal is a court set up by a competent authority to ascertain facts, judge an issue and advise, recommend, or order a course of action. Tribunals have been established by military and ecclesiastical authorities to judge and punish offenders against military or ecclesiastical regulations: they were set up by the revolutionaries during the French Revolution to determine the fate of citizens accused of being counter-revolutionaries; and local tribunals have been set up in England to hear claims for exemption from military service.

The reliability and effectiveness of a tribunal depends on its terms of reference and powers, as well as the integrity of the judges or other individuals appointed to serve on it. The combination of judicial with executive power (the accuser acting also as judge) is a serious defect. While capable of

188

making rapid decisions, tribunals are liable to be biassed, and trial by tribunal is unsatisfactory unless there is at least the right of appeal to an independent higher court.

Law
2. In English law, a tribunal may be set up under the 1921 Act by the Prime Minister with the approval of Parliament to inquire into any matter of public concern. It may be appointed to ascertain facts but not to apportion blame. A tribunal of this kind has the power to compel attendance of witnesses for examination on oath or on affirmation and the power to compel the production of documents. Refusal could incur a charge for contempt of court. It can also issue a request to a foreign Government to examine a witness abroad. But such a tribunal is not a court of law and it does not have the power to commit for contempt any person not ordered to appear before the tribunal. It is therefore possible for the press to report and comment on the inquiry while it is in progress.

UNCONSCIOUS

Common Language
As an adjective, 'unconsious' means unaware, a state in which no sensory impressions are received and in which there are no subjective experiences, as in coma or in sleep.

Psychology
Freud put forward the concept that consciousness is based on and emerges from a large store of hidden motive and ideas of which we are normally unaware and which constitute the *unconscious*. He considered that all our conscious mental processes have their origin in the unconscious, which is largely infantile in character, egocentric, sexually oriented, and directed towards obtaining pleasure and avoiding trouble and pain. 'The Unconscious represents within each of us the infant, the primitive man and also the animal' (Crichton-Miller). Freud also developed the view that the unconscious may include thoughts, wishes and ideas which are repressed from consciousness because

189

they are painful in nature and therefore unacceptable. A person's behaviour is influenced by factors of that kind, but since they are removed from consciousness he does not normally know they exist. They can however be brought to light and made conscious by procedures such as those of psychoanalysis. Unconscious factors influencing behaviour can be the underlying cause of mental symptoms such as hallucinactions and hysteria, and these can be cured by bringing into consciousness their unconscious causes.

UNDERWRITING

Economics
1. Accepting a part of the risk of an insurance, by guaranteeing to pay, in return for a premium, a specified sum in the event of loss. In a large transaction, such as the insurance of a ship or of a valuable cargo, it is usual to spread the risk over a number of different underwriters who state the proportion of the total risk they are willing to bear by writing their initials on a 'slip' describing the ship or other object that is being insured. Those who wish to insure property generally deal with the underwriters through a broker or insurance agent.

The largest British association of underwriters known as Lloyd's, takes its name from a certain Edward Lloyd who ran a coffee-house at which merchants of the City of London used to meet in 1688. The underwriters at Lloyd's do not claim the protection accorded to limited liability companies, but each underwriter holds himself personally liable for the risks he undertakes. Lloyd's were orignally concerned with British marine insurance, but their business is now largely international and covers practically every kind of insurance risk except life insurance.

2. Agreeing to buy a specified proportion of new shares issued by a company in the event of their not being bought by the public. The underwriters thereby ensure that the whole of an issue of new capital will be taken up.

UNIVERSAL

Common Language
The universe is all that exists, including the solar and stellar systems; and the adjective *universal* means in every case, in every place, applicable without exception.

Philosophy
1. A universal is a generalisation applicable to all cases, which are thus held to be of the same kind as members of the same class. It is a concept abstracted by our thinking from a number of particular instances; for example, all triangles have three sides.
2. A universal is an attribute, a quality or characteristic which can be affirmed as a property of every member of a specific class. For example, 'all children are naughty'.
3. A universal is one of the five general classes of attributes defined by Aristotle, namely the *predictables*.

VALUE

Common Language
The value of anything is its relative worth, usefulness, desirability or importance with respect to a particular reference scale which needs to be specified if the meaning of the word is to be clear. The value of an object in economic terms is given by the quantity of other objects that can be obtained in exchange, and this may be indicated by its monetary value or the purchase price: but the purchasing power of money can change, so that the price cannot be regarded as a permanent indication of value. An object may also have an *aesthetic value* or a *sentimental value* which cannot be easily assessed in economic terms.

Maths
The value of an algebraic symbol or expression is the number or quantity it represents.

Music
In a musical composition the value of a note is its relative length or duration.

VANDALISM

Common Language
Vandalism means deliberately damaging objects which are of value. The word comes from the name of the Vandal tribe who invaded Europe in the fifth Century AD and who through ignorance and lack of appreciation destroyed many fine buildings and works of art. The objects damaged by vandals are usually public property rather than property privately owned, and vandals are often young and immature.

Sociology
Acts of vandalism often appear to be meaningless and irrational. Those responsible for such acts have sometimes been regarded as mentally deranged, but there is generally a motive behind their acts which is related to their cultural background. Recognisable motives include: (i) greed, as in damaging slot machines to get money from them, (ii) self-assertion, or the desire to show courage in accepting the challenge of doing what is forbidden, (iii) vindictiveness, to express a sense of grievance or settle a debt, (iv) malice, as an expression of anger, (v) play, as when children go smashing windows, (vi) scheming, as when work in a factory can be stopped by damaging machines. Vandalism may serve as an escape from boredom, resentment, frustration or failure.

Art
The word 'vandalism' is sometimes used in a figurative sense to define an attitude or coarseness, lack of refinements, or hostility to beauty.

VECTOR

Biology
1. The word vector comes from the Latin *vehere* to carry. A

192

vector is an animal that conveys a living organism between different animal hosts of another species. Thus a mosquito (*anopheles*) is a vector in carrying the malarial parasite from one human host to another.

If the organism carried undergoes an essential phase of its life cycle in the vector, the vector is known as a *biological vector*: the vector is described as a *passive* or *mechanical vector* when the organism carried undergoes no essential change. Vectors are important factors in the spread of many kinds of disease in animals and in man.

Mathematics

2. A vector is a quantity that has direction as well as size: it is a directed magnitude. Thus velocity and force are vector quantities. A vector may be represented graphically by an arrow, in which the length gives the magnitude, and the angle with respect to a system of coordinates gives the direction of the vector.

3. A *radius vector* is a variable straight line extending from a fixed point (the origin) to a curve. Thus in astronomy a vector is an imaginary straight line joining a satellite to the centre of the circle or focus of the ellipse in which it revolves.

Statistics

4. Vectors are used in statistical analysis as a method of expressing data that can be defined in terms of quantities having direction as well as size (magnitude). Thus the resultant influence of a number of different factors operating in producing a particular effect can be assessed by representing the individual factors as having different directions as well as lengths. In this way the resultant may be determined.

Psychology

5. Vectors are used for the systematic delineation and representation of the psychological factors operating in any particular situation. The test score of an individual factor is represented by the length of a vector. The correlation between any two factors is represented by the angle between two vectors, where the cosine of the angle gives the

correlation coefficient. Two vectors at right angles therefore have a zero correlation; and the smaller the angle between any two vectors, the higher the correlation coefficient.

VEGETARIAN

Common Language
A vegetarian is a person who eats only a vegetarian diet. Vegetarian diets include fruit and vegetables, but mostly they exclude all meat. They vary considerably in other respects. Most vegetarian diets, while excluding meat, include eggs, milk, butter, cheese and sometimes fish. Generally they provide all the normal human dietary requirements, but diets restricted to vegetables only and excluding all animal products can lead to ill health due to deficiency of vitamin B_{12}. Individuals who eat vegetables only, known as *vegans*, sometimes become anaemic and they may suffer from irritability, depression, headache and other symptoms. It may be said that some vegetarian diets are healthy while others are not.

VIOLENCE

Common Language
1. The primary meaning of violence is the exercise of physical force in a way that can cause personal injury, as in wounding or assault. (2) Violence also means causing damage to property, as in vandalism or bombing. (3) In a wider sense of the word, violence is behaviour which can cause a severe emotional reaction, such as a direct threat to use physical force or to do damage.

The significance of the word 'violence' varies greatly, depending on the underlying motive, the circumstances and the extent of the injury inflicted. Behaviour such as assault or killing is *criminal violence* if motivated by anger, greed or the wish to take revenge, but it may be regarded by some as fully justified if done for military, legal, political or religious reasons. It may then be described as an act of 'punishment', 'restraint', or 'defence'.

4. An extended meaning of violence is fury or vehemence, as in the violence of a hurricane, a thunderstorm, a violent passion, or violent criticism. (5) Another meaning of violence is excessive misuse, as in the profanation of what is sacred or 'doing violence to' an accepted principle. Violence is not a homogeneous type of human behaviour. Armed robbery, murder of a wife's lover, vandalism and a boxing match are all violent activities, but they differ widely in nature.

Medicine
Some people are more aggressive than others. There are violent individuals who when frustrated can burst into a devastating rage and commit an act of violence. There are others who readily become violent after taking alcohol. From a medical point of view it is important to know whether a person's violence is attributable to pathological factors and whether they are of a kind that can be treated or not. It is recognized that some individuals known as *psychomotor epileptics* can commit acts of violence when they have a siezure, and that may be brought on by a high fluid intake, as by drinking more than two pints of liquid. This condition can be established by examing the electrical activity of the brain with an electroencephalograph (EEG), and some cases can be treated effectively by the administration of a suitable anti-epileptic drug. Animal research with monkeys has shown that aggressive behaviour commonly depends on the activity of a small part of the brain known as the amygdala, and it can be prevented by surgical operation of amygdalectomy. Japanese surgeons have now used amygdalectomy for the treatment of prisoners who have committed acts of criminal violence. Their reports indicate that most of the patients treated in that way were improved, but this form of treatment is not in general use, since the official adoption of such treatment would raise serious ethical problems.

Law
When a prisoner charged with criminal violence is brought to trial in Court a question frequently asked is whether he was resposible for his acts or whether he was suffering from

a form of mental disorder which would allow a verdict of diminished responsibility. In a classical case of a youth of seventeen who raped and murdered an elderly woman of seventy-five the judge accepted medical evidence that the youth suffered from psychomoter epilepsy and the charge of murder was dropped. Evidence of mental disorder now plays an important part in the defence of prisoners charged with violence.

Sociology
A natural response to violence is often that of moral revulsion and desire for revenge. Thus violence tends to engender violence. However, attitudes taken towards violence depend very much on the cultural background. In many communities there are sub-cultures which differ in their norms and values from the main central culture, and which show a greater readiness to accept the standards involved in behaviour such as football hooliganism or gang violence. In such sub-cultures qualities such as toughness, virility, risk-taking or 'aggro' can serve as criteria for group acceptance, and in social interaction a violent response may be expected or even required. The language of violence therefore has a different significance in sub-cultures in which status depends on the ability to fight. In civilised societies the response to violence is tempered by the rules of law and order.

See VANDALISM.

VIVISECTION

Common Language
Vivisection is the performance of experiments on living animals. The word literally means 'live cutting' and vivisection is commonly taken to mean operating surgically on living mammals such as cats, dogs and monkeys in ways that cause pain and disfigurement or death. Animal experiments of all kinds are opposed by anti-vivisectionists, who insist on the cruelty of the procedure and hold that it is unjust that animals should be made to suffer for the benefit of men. The results achieved by vivisection, as in obtaining

scientific information or the testing of cosmetics, are regarded by them as little value and in the UK anti-vivisectionists demand that *all* experiments on living animals should be prohibited.

Biology
Vivisections signifies a wide range of different procedures which include not only surgical operations on anaesthetised animals, but also the injection of drugs, feeding experiments and other procedures, many of which cause little or no pain. The animals most generally used in vivisection are rats and mice specially bred for the purpose. In the UK vivisection is controlled by the Cruelty to Animals Act which prohibits animal experiments liable to cause severe pain. Vivisecton may be performed on vertebrate animals only by licensed individuals with appropriate scientific qualifications, and they may be carried out only in specially licensed laboratories which are regularly visited by Home Office Inspectors.

The amount of scientific information obtained by vivisection experiments is very great, and vivisection has resulted in major discoveries of special value in medical science. It is widely used for such puposes as the testing of drugs and vaccines. Vivisection has made possible the development of a number of effective new methods of treatment of disease and it has thereby saved many human lives. It has also led to the development of new and effective methods of veterinary treatment of animals. Diseases which can now be prevented or cured as a result of vivisection experiments include rabies, smallpox, typhoid, cholera and plague.

WILL

Common Language
1. Will is the mental faculty which controls our voluntary thoughts and actions and which therefore determines the general direction of our behaviour. Willed or voluntary actions may be contrasted with involuntary, unwilled, spontaneous or reflex actions such as blinking or yawning; but the degree of voluntariness can vary and the distinction

is not always clear. Thus skilled activities such as knitting or typing can be continued with little or no conscious or voluntary effort while a person's thoughts are otherwise engaged, and a pianist can carry on animated conversation while playing the piano.
2. Will is the wish, determination, or action of willing to do something: the conscious intention that something shall be done.
3. A will is a document or formal declaration giving the way in which people wish their property to be disposed of after their death.

Psychology
4. Schopenhauer drew a distinction between a person's intellect and their will, which he regarded as made up of a variety of irrational and emotional impulses.

WISDOM

Common Language
1. Wisdom is the specific attribute of one who is wise. It implies qualities such as sound judgment based on extensive knowledge, wide experience, high intellectual ability, sanity, a sense of proportion, deep understanding and mature reflection. While *common sense* is the ability to deal with current problems in a skillful and sensible way as judged by popular consensus, wisdom has a deeper meaning in being a basic guide to behaviour at a more fundamental level, especially in matters relating to the conduct of life. It is an attribute of distinction which is respected by all.
2. Wisdom can mean a set of teachings free from personal prejudice, implying more than knowledge alone and representing the broad outlook and considered views of those who are held to be wise.

WORK. WORKER

Common Language
1. Work is physical or mental *exertion*, or labour directed

198

towards a specific end, as in housework, gardening, studying or earning a living.

2. Work is a specific job, a task requiring effort and skill. In this sense of the word it has been said that 'work is dignity, the only real dignity' (Scott Fitzgerald). The meaning of the word in any specific context depends on the nature of the work and hence on the goal: this may be to make money, or to satisfy some specific need. Work may be regarded as irksome and unrewarding ('the curse of Adam') or it may be enjoyed; but activities performed mainly for pleasure are commonly regarded not as work, but rather as recreation or play.

3. In a more restricted sense of the word work is *paid* employment, as distinct from unpaid or voluntary work. Thus a person who is unemployed may be said to have no work, even if actively engaged in tasks of other kinds.

4. Work is the *product* of purposeful physical or mental effort, as for example an earthwork, a literary or scientific work, needlework or a work of art.

5. The plural 'works', is commonly used for (a) the essential mechanical part of an instrument, as in the works of a clock. It is also used for (b) a factory or department where work is carried out.

A *worker* is literally (a) anyone who does work of any kind, as a cloth-worker, hand-worker, brain-worker, etc. The word can be used when expressed with emphasis to indicate (b) a person who works hard and effectively, as distinct from others who are idle or inclined to waste time. The word 'worker' has also been used in a restricted sense for (c) manual labourers and those engaged in more lowly employment, who are regarded as belonging to the *working classes*. In this sense of the word a social distinction is implied between the underprivileged workers and the upper-class managers, directors, higher civil servants, professional people and others who live at a higher income level ('Workers of the world unite! You have nothing to lose but your chains' Communist Mauifesto). However, in more recent years the social distinction between those working at different income levels has become increasingly blurred.

A *workshop* is (a) a room or building where work is carried out by manual workers. It can also mean (b) a teaching seminar for the communication of practical working techniques.

Physiology
6. Work is the energy expended in physical exertion. It may be measured in calories.

Physics
7. Work is done when a force (P) acts through a distance (L) to cause movement or other physical change. The dimensions of work are force multiplied by length (PL). A practical unit of work is the *foot-pound*, which is the work done by a force of one pound acting through the distance of one foot. In the centimetre-gram-second system of units the unit of work is the *erg*, which is the work done by a force of one dyne acting through a distance of one centimetre. The electrical unit of work, the *joule*, is the work done when a current of one ampère flows against a resistance of one ohm for one second.